Jane Cumberbatch's
Recipes for Every Day

For Alastair, Tom, Georgie, Gracie
and my parents John and Jean

First published in the United Kingdom in 2010 by
Pavilion Books, Old West London Magistrates Court,
10 Southcombe Street, London W14 0RA

An imprint of Anova Books Company Ltd

Design and layout © Pavilion, 2010
Text © Jane Cumberbatch 2010
Photography © Vanessa Courtier 2010
Illustration © Grace Brown
Other images © see acknowledgements p 272

Publisher: Anna Cheifetz
Cookery, Growing, Sewing, Making and Styling: Jane Cumberbatch
Marketing and Personal Assistant: Patricia Gill
Photography and Design: Vanessa Courtier
Copy Editor: Jackie Moseley
Illustrations: Grace Brown
Index: Hilary Bird

ISBN 978-1-86205-912-2

A CIP catalogue record for this book is available from the British Library.

2 4 6 8 10 9 7 5 3 1

Reproduction by Rival Colour Ltd, UK
Printed and bound by 1010 Printing International Ltd, China

www.anovabooks.com

Jane Cumberbatch's
Recipes for Every Day

photography by Vanessa Courtier

PAVILION

contents

introduction

I love to cook, to garden and to make things. This book is a visual and written notebook of my ideas and recipes, spanning the seasons and including the ways in which I try to make daily life as simple and pleasing as possible. Some people are hard-wired to do complicated algorithms or run marathons, but I can't imagine a life without making things and putting my stamp on something. I suppose it's my way of making sense of the world, of keeping some control. There's not much we can do about the big stuff, but there's an awful lot we can do that's satisfying, such as baking a cake, growing some beans, or giving a new look to a piece of furniture with a lick of paint.

This book is very much part of my Pure Style philosophy, which is about being economical without skimping on essential things such as good food. It is not all about slavishly following fashion. It's about being practical and resourceful and it's about enjoying all the good things in a simpler way. I want the reader to be inspired, just as I am, by the ordinary and everyday aspects of life, such as making toast or cutting a rose.

Putting all of the following words, pictures and ideas into context, I should say that it all started with my mum, who taught me how to make everything from a sponge cake to a summer dress for school. Along the way, I've been like a kind of design sponge, absorbing ideas wherever I've seen or read about something that thrills me

I'd like to say, too, that everything in this book has been (or is being) test-driven by me and my family in homes that have ranged from a rickety Georgian terrace house in east London to a bleached white farmhouse in southern Spain to our current home, with its old-fashioned roses and tall Victorian sash windows. My ongoing passion and project, for further inspiration and lessons in cooking the perfect sardine, is another white-washed space that we are restoring in Olhão, a salty seaside fishing town in the Algarve, Portugal.

Jane Cumberbatch

Good things to eat in spring: rhubarb, leeks, purple sprouting broccoli, spring greens, new potatoes, carrots, asparagus, spring lamb, mackerel, oysters, watercress, broad beans, wild garlic, elderflower, eggs.

spring

What bliss it is when I can first walk barefoot on the grass and lie face up in the sun's warming rays. Listening to a blackbird singing its heart out or soaking up the visual balm of a tree in blossom lessens the sting of a parking ticket or some other urban irritant. In his book *In Praise of Slow*[1], Carl Honoré exorts us to slow down and seek to live at what musicians call *tempo giusto* – the right speed. It's about trying to live better in a fast-paced modern world. Paying attention to what is going on in the renewal of nature – watching the buds pushing upwards or limp leaves unfurling, for example – is a simple pleasure that is free and a world away from consumer hype.

SWEET BROAD BEANS
AND LIME GREEN SHOOTS

'Spring is when life's alive in everything.'
Christina Rossetti

Against the garden's winter wreckage, green shoots poking through the earth are optimistic signs of spring where only four weeks ago a white blanket of snow lay. After months of nature's inertia, suddenly everything seems possible. I can even find the motivation to sort through and dust down the dark innards of the larder: bailing out the dregs of jam jars and cereal boxes; clearing away saggy sweet potatoes, tired onions and other vegetables that I haven't been quite as organized at using up as I should have been; and putting in order the muddle of cans, packets, bags of rice and pulses. I feel productive and energized, as if coming out of hibernation.

**A first day of
spring risotto**
serves 4–6

(see page 165 for
Mushroom risotto)

In tune with the spring mood, what we love to eat is risotto with green peas, broad beans and asparagus. This one is inspired by the classic Italian *risotto primavera*.

It's best if you can lay your hands on fresh pods but frozen peas (petit pois are sweetest) and frozen young broad beans are acceptable. And if the asparagus element is impossible (it might not be available or you might not feel justified in using airfreighted spears), you can just leave it out and add a few more peas and beans. Try to use a heavy-based saucepan to stop the rice sticking and a wooden spoon for the vigorous stirring that is the key to a successful risotto.

1½ tbsp olive oil
75g/3oz/¾ stick unsalted butter
1 onion, finely chopped
6 spring onions, finely chopped
2 garlic cloves, chopped
300g/10oz/scant 1½ cups risotto rice
150ml/¼ pint/⅔ cup white wine

1.2 litres/2 pints/5 cups hot chicken or vegetable stock
8 asparagus spears, chopped into 2cm (¾-inch) pieces
200g/7oz/1¾ cups shelled peas
200g/7oz/1½ cups shelled broad beans
fresh mint leaves, torn
50g/2oz/½ cup grated Parmesan cheese
sea salt and freshly ground black pepper

Heat the oil and half the butter. Add the onion, spring onions and garlic and cook over a medium heat for about 10 minutes until soft. Add the rice and stir for a couple of minutes to coat the grains in oil. Add the wine and start adding the hot stock a ladleful at a time, stirring continuously (resist pleas, however plaintive, for help with homework, or from a hungry dog – stirring is the key to a good risotto).

After 15 minutes add the asparagus and keep stirring and adding stock for 5 more minutes. Add the remaining vegetables and cook the bubbling and steaming contents for a further 5 minutes, adding the stock as necessary.

It's ready when the rice goes creamy, but not to the point of soggy; the grains should retain a chewy al dente quality. Turn off the heat. Season to taste with salt and freshly ground black pepper, stir in the remaining butter and the torn mint leaves and leave to rest for a few minutes with the lid on.

Serve with grated Parmesan, ideally immediately, but if you are thwarted by domestic drama, don't worry – the risotto will not be a disaster if it sits in the pan for another 15 minutes or so.

A new look for spring

The simplest thing you can do to change the look in your space is to give it a new coat of paint.

Now that spring has sprung and sunlight is dancing all over the house again I can see just how grimy and grubby everything is, especially in the kitchen. There's no need for home to be the perfect domestic palace, but equally a greasy oven isn't exactly uplifting. So, like retouching grey roots, a spot of simple spring-cleaning can be a brilliant reviver of the spirits, as well as keeping everything in good nick.

Nowadays of course we must use bleach and other noxious cleaning materials only sparingly, but a simple bucket of hot water, a little detergent and a sponge is the underpinning for dealing with most tasks.

There is also satisfaction in having a good sweep with a bristle broom or making mirrors sparkle with a rag soaked in vinegar. I might even pursue the idea from a 19th-century guide to domesticity that suggested sweeping with tea leaves 'not only to lay the dust but also to give a slightly fragrant smell to the room'.

Some Simple Colours

pale lavender
in a sitting room
is restful

cool grey for
simple urban
rooms

Country cream
for a cottage kitchen

Lime green a
perfect foil for
chocolate or pinks

green blues
look good in the
kitchen and garden

Olive green
for sheds and fences

Cobalt blue : a
seaside colour

hyacinth blue :
pretty for bedrooms

Violet looks
good with pinks
& greens

Stone : a good
colour for period
houses

terracotta :
for a snug feel
in a sitting room
or study

Yellow walls
look good with
green/blue details

Good uses for distilled white vinegar:

window cleaner
fabric softener
air freshener
stain remover
weedkiller
loo cleaner
drain cleaner
wallpaper remover
grease cutter
furniture polish
limescale remover
glue solvent

Good uses for apple cider vinegar:
nit remover
treatment for sunburn
ear cleaner
insect repellent
relief for stings

Going back to the greasy oven – say goodbye to suffocating foam – it can be made wholesome and shiny again with non-toxic cleaners or even your own eco paste made from borax and water. And if, like me, you have open shelving for plates and glasses above the cooker, the whole lot will need a good wash after a winter of roasts and cheese on toast. For this task, and all other washing up, I can't think of anything better than tough white and blue striped linen tea towels.

And if I don't have the inclination or energy to do any of the above, it's enough simply to fling the windows wide open and let out the fug to give my mood a boost.

In the same way that the female whitewashers in Andalucia appear with the first wild peonies, as the sticky buds unfurl like limp chickens' feet in Tulse Hill, south London, it's time for me to get out my painting shirt.

How to paint

The days are longer, putty and other materials are not in danger of setting too hard to work with, and if it's an outside job there's hopefully less chance of rain stopping play. Like learning how to bake a cake, or any other basic cooking task, it is very useful to learn how to paint.

Dip the brush in the paint to cover half the bristle length. Wipe off any excess paint on the side of the tin. Lay the paint on by applying a horizontal band approximately 20cm (8 inches) wide and brush it out sideways.

Finish with light strokes in a criss-cross pattern. Hold a small paintbrush like a pencil but hold a large paintbrush like a beach bat.

If using a roller, load it with paint by pushing it back and forth in the front of the tray, then do the same on the slope of the tray to spread the paint evenly over the roller. Roll slowly and evenly until the area is covered.

All about colour

The theory of colour can be as off-putting as a long-winded recipe in a fancy cookbook for something as simple as tomato soup. Why make life more convoluted than it already is? It is enough to say here that the light-reflecting qualities of colour are the most significant.

Here are some key pointers: Think carefully about the aspect of a room. North-facing rooms are darker and need warm colours such as soft yellows. South-facing rooms can have harsh shadows so cooler blues and greens will work well. Rooms facing east are warmer in the morning with more yellow light from the sunrise, which cools as the day progresses. Walls that have direct light appear light and walls that surround a window fall into shadow so colours will appear darker.

Some green rooms

What with all the buds in the garden and delicious greens in the vegetable basket, it's easy to get inspired about using leafy hues around the home. It might be obvious, but it is because of its association with nature that green is one of the most accommodating colours for interiors. And when described on the paint charts with tempting culinary imagery, such as 'pea', 'cooking-apple green', 'bean', and 'cabbage', a green theme is even more inviting.

Go easy on the light, bright end of the green spectrum – perfect for a hyacinth stalk, acidic lime green all over a room is hard on the eye and stomach. Duller greens that make me think of olives or a field in winter are timeless, quiet and look as good in a country cottage as in a more modern environment. White bed linen or chair covers look crisp and fresh against these more muted green shades.

Recently I painted a north-facing room (see page 14) in a deep citrine green, which I was worried about embarking on, being such a lover of white, but the effect is rich and enveloping, almost like being in the garden. This use of wraparound colour in one shade creates continuity and has made the proportions of this small room actually seem larger. To introduce some contrast I have used paler shades of a blue-green to paint chairs and a simple junk table.

Greens look great in the kitchen, too. I recommend a pale chalky mint green as a soothing backdrop for cooking and working.

Wild things

The bedding is airing under a sheet of blue sky and I have flung open every door and window to blow away months of fustiness. This is the sort of day to go out with a pair of scissors to snip a handful of wild garlic or young nettle heads. Add to this the hunter-gatherer pleasure of returning with a fistful of greenery for the pot.

Wild garlic soup
(see page 15)

Abundant in country woods, it's not unusual in spring to find the fresh green and white froth of wild garlic – ransoms – in a suburban back garden. My brother-in-law Jonny's dad lives in north London and he has a shady spot by the shed with a useful carpet of this garlicky-scented greenery. Eat wild garlic leaves raw in salads or as a garnish (wash well in case the dog, cat, badger or fox has decorated them in passing). The leaves will keep for several days in the refrigerator, but they bruise easily so handle gently.

Alternative uses for wild garlic:

Substitute wild garlic for basil in a pesto (see page 110). You can also cook it as you would spinach and enjoy it as a vegetable, or chop and mix with home-made beef burgers (see page 125).

25g/1oz/¼ stick unsalted butter
2 leeks, trimmed and roughly chopped
1.2 litres/2 pints/5 cups vegetable stock
1kg/2lb potatoes, peeled and roughly chopped
generous handful of wild garlic leaves, well washed and roughly chopped
3–4 tbsp crème fraîche
sea salt and freshly ground black pepper

Melt the butter in a heavy-based saucepan and cook the chopped leeks gently for 5 minutes until soft. Add the stock and simmer on a medium heat for about 10 minutes. Add the potatoes and simmer for a further 15-20 minutes, or until they are just cooked through.

Blend half the soup, either in a liquidizer or with a hand-held blender, then pour back into the soup. This gives it a chunky consistency; for a smoother texture, liquidize the whole lot.

Add the wild garlic and simmer for a few more minutes. Season to taste and serve with dollops of crème fraîche.

Nettle soup

I pick young green nettles when they're a fizz of pale green leaves sprouting through still bare patches of wintry ground. This is when they're at their tenderest.

Expert instructions from the 'Dig for Victory' campaign in World War II:

'To gather them without being stung you can wear an old glove between February and June. Put them into a pail under your tap and twirl them around well using a piece of wood – when the nettles are thoroughly wet, they lose the power of stinging you. There is no fear of them stinging the throat once boiling water has touched them.'

1 tbsp olive oil
2 onions, finely chopped
2 garlic cloves, finely chopped
1.2 litres/2 pints/5 cups vegetable stock
500g/1lb potatoes, peeled and finely chopped
2 gloved handfuls of young nettle heads, washed
150ml/¼ pint/⅔ cup double cream
salt and freshly ground black pepper

Heat the olive oil and cook the onions and garlic in a heavy-based saucepan for 5 minutes or so, until soft. Add the stock and simmer for 10 minutes.

Add the potatoes and nettles (do remember the gloves) and simmer for a further 10 minutes or so until the potatoes are tender.

Liquidize, season to taste, and stir in the cream.

Elderflower fizz
makes about 2 litres

Back in the 1970s my dad and uncle were always experimenting with homemade brews using the recycled bottles from the box in the shed. My father's blackberry wine was dangerously alcoholic, but my uncle's elderflower champagne was lethal: when I uncorked one bottle, such was the build-up of pressure that the neck broke and neatly sliced off part of my thumb. Happily, no such disaster occurred with my first attempt at making this fragrant and lightly fizzy drink, as I stuck to strong screw-top wine bottles, and let the pressure off every couple of days.

Elders
Elders are found in gardens, parks and on commons and waste ground. Flowering in late April and May, the delicate white blooms should be gathered when just out of bud.

2 litres/3½ pints/8 cups boiling water
500g/1lb/2½ cups granulated or caster sugar
rind and juice of 4 lemons
10 elderflower heads, in full bloom

Put the water and sugar into a clean bucket and stir until the sugar dissolves.

Add the lemon rind and juice and the elderflower heads and stir. Cover with clean muslin or a linen tea towel and leave to ferment in a cool place for 4–5 days.

Strain the liquid through a sieve lined with muslin and decant into sterilized strong glass bottles.

Wild asparagus

Although it is now protected in the UK, rough-tied, flopping bunches of wild asparagus are still a feature in the spring markets of Spain and Portugal. Foraging for wild asparagus *espárragos trigueros* among the hedgerows of the Sierra needs a sharp eye and is a fun way to teach children how to be more observant. The thin pencil-like spears are easily confused with grass if you don't look hard. They are like spindly versions of the cultivated stuff we normally eat.

Dandelion leaves

Before the pet rabbit gets them, follow the old French kitchen-garden tradition and pick the first young spring dandelion leaves to throw into a salad.

Ground elder

It is an understatement that many gardeners would wish worldwide annihilation of this rampant plant but if you can keep it relatively tamed, why not appreciate its pretty frothing white flower heads. The leaves can be steamed like spinach, eaten raw in salads or added to soups.

THE BEAUTIFUL AND USEFUL GARDEN

It occurs to me that William Morris's tenet *'Have nothing in your house that you do not know to be useful, or believe to be beautiful'* applies just as much to the garden as it does to the home. Fancy garden fashions come and go – leylandii, pampas grass, stripy lawns, decking and chained pergolas to name but a few horrors – but the most timeless kind of gardening is like timeless interior decoration: simple, natural and unpretentious. I am all for what the Japanese call *'wabi-sabi'*, which identifies beauty with unpretentious, simple, unfinished, transient things. So there is *'wabi-sabi'* in plain buckets, in walls with blemishes and in rough weathered stones covered with lichen. As a *'wabi-sabi'* devotee you won't find me using high-pressure hoses to remove the moss from the brick in my back garden.

When you're planning your outside space, think of it as a room outside with a background canvas to highlight and complement whatever you plant in it. It goes without saying that the more natural the textures, the better. You might be lucky and have lovely old brick walls, or a classic cottage hedge. It's more likely, though, to be some kind of fencing which, even if it is in an unappealing varnish, can be updated with colour. It will look more natural if you choose muted greens rather than anything too bright and loud. This isn't a design rule written in stone, but you might find that an electric blue background may be fine for a Miami patio, but will look out of place in the softer light that we have in the UK.

I discovered the ideal green in a water-based paint from Cuprinol, which has become my default garden colour. Slapped on with a wide brush, across a muddle of mismatched trellis and fencing, it creates a simple unified backdrop to flowers and plants. This is the garden as a room outside.

Grand gardens are breathtaking and magnificent. If you can, do visit the baked and shady gardens of the Alcazar in Seville, Spain or Vita Sackville-West's languorous borders at Sissinghurst in Kent. But I am also drawn to more humble, informal and personal creations such as the traditional cottage garden with its mingling of ornamental and useful elements. This is the old-as-the-hills idea of

Some spring gardening tasks:

Sow hardy annuals outdoors.

Sow half-hardy annuals under cover.

Cover emerging shoots with fleece.

Sort seeds for sowing.

Sow broad beans outside.

Feed shrubs and climbers with a slow-release organic feed and work in bonemeal.

Prune roses with sharp secateurs; remove a percentage of old wood where you can to promote new wood, as a vigorous plant is less prone to disease.

Divide perennials such as agapanthus to make more plants: cut down the middle of the clump and prise apart with two forks before replanting. Slower-growing clump-forming perennials such as peonies can be left for many years before they decline. Prise the most vigorous outer sections away with a fork for replanting (you can also do this in autumn).

Trench the vegetable beds, and dig in compost or manure.

Hoe to keep up with the weeds.

Clear the beds of last year's skeletons.

self-sufficiency. It's a timeless way, too, when you see that what worked for one medieval gardening guru, the monk Alexander Needham, is just as relevant today for anyone planning a herb, vegetable and flower garden. *The English Cottage Garden* by Edward Haymans[2] records he dictated that: '*The garden should be adorned with roses and lilies, turnsole, violets and mandrake; there you should have parsley and cos, and fennel and southernwood and coriander, sage, savory, hyssop, mint, rue, dittany, smallage, pellitory, lettuce, garden cress, peonies. There should also be planted beds with onions, leeks, garlic, pumpkins and shallots, cucumber, poppy, daffodil and acanthus ought to be in a good garden. There should also be pottage herbs such as beets, herb mercury, orach, sorrel and mallows.*'

My mum had much of the medieval monk approach to our south London suburban garden, practising the wartime resourcefulness of her parents. There were raspberry canes squeezed between the roses, courgettes next to more herbs, and tubs of ripening tomatoes piled along a south-facing wall at the back of the house.

As a nascent gardener I followed, and armed with her wisdom, *The Gardening Year* by Reader's Digest, and bargain trays of plants from the Sunday flower market in London's Columbia Road, I crammed a postage-stamp-sized roof terrace with herbs, sweet peas and clematis against a backdrop of crumbling east London sheds and warehouses. My very English garden theme continued, with the addition of a good hat, high in the Andalucian Sierra, where – despite ferocious summer heat and freezing winters – climbing white roses, old-fashioned scented geraniums and sweet white jasmine flowers bloomed profusely around the white courtyard walls.

Now that we're UK based, I can concentrate on the long skinny vegetable patch in the sunniest part of the garden by the fence and my loose interpretation of an old-fashioned potager – a patchwork effect made of 16 small beds edged with recycled Victorian tiles and planted with rows of lavender and rosemary.

It is laid out with four standard rose trees in the middle and wigwams of climbing beans and nasturtiums at each corner. Pathways laid with shingle gravel between the beds are wide enough to fit a wheelbarrow. It is formal, yet informal, and can be quite out of hand without looking too much of a mess.

The aim is to always have something edible or beautiful, or both, out there. At the very least, I'll always have herbs to cook with, or to put in jugs for greenery at the table, even in the middle of winter, when the garden is stark and bare on the flower side of things.

In defence of weeds

'A weed is no more than a flower in disguise.' James Russell Lowell, American romantic poet and writer

**Favourite
wild things:**

Bluebells: gorgeous porcelain-blue colour and heady scent – a 'strong sweet smell, somewhat stuffing the head' said the herbalist John Gerard. Juices from the plant stiffened Elizabethan ruffs, and glue from the flower stalks has been used for binding books or fixing feathers on arrows.

Lesser celandine: known as the 'spring messenger', it's a pretty yellow flower like a glossy buttercup, a favourite of the Flame Brocade moth, and once used for treating piles.

White dead-nettle: delicate white orchid-like flowers – described by John Gerard as a plant 'to make the heart merry'. Children used to make whistles from the stems, and in the north-east of England the leaves were often fed to young turkeys.

As with dealing with a backlog of greasy dishes, it's a chore to hack through the brambles and suckers that threaten to choke the flower beds. On the other hand (in my misguided opinion, as the more serious garden-minded will probably think) there are what I call the 'right' kind of weeds, which are as much a part of the garden as my pampered, old-fashioned roses.

I have no desire, therefore, to zap the sunny-coloured dandelions and the white daisies that decorate the glossy, velvety spring grass. Nor the clumps of cabbagey forget-me-nots, whose tiny and piercing cobalt-blue flowers are perfect for a simple table decoration with white dead-nettles. I love the gentle disorder and interest that the right kind of weeds can bring to the garden, like colourful gatecrashers at a formal party. And even scrubby patches of urban wasteland get their chance to bloom, in spring especially, as unexpected oases of wild beauty.

I prefer to think that weeds are just plants growing in the wrong place. Anyway, they have an entitlement to be doing all their growing as the descendants of naturally occurring wild flowers and plants. Our forebears, who were so much closer to nature, had a greater need of wild plants and linked them with superstitions and special powers. A culture of plant lore flourished, such as using feverfew against headaches and not taking hawthorn blossom into the house because it brings bad luck.

But any green invader has its limits. The overuse of fertilizers in the countryside has resulted in the stinging nettle being the most common plant in the English countryside because it can tolerate high levels of nitrogen. This is at the expense of more delicate plants, which are fighting to survive. Making more nettle soup (see page 18) will not exactly address the problem, but we can have a go.

And although I'm no xenophobe, there are some plant experts who are convinced that foreign plants are pushing Britain's wild flowers to extinction. Apparently nine of the ten fastest-spreading species were recently introduced from abroad. Some plants, such as the fen orchid and pennyroyal, barely survive outside nature reserves and SSSI (Sites of Special Scientific Interest). Even the cornflower is listed as endangered.

You can do your bit for native plants in your garden or allotment, and sow a bed of wild flowers to attract bees, butterflies and other insects. *This is one typical meadow mix from a packet of seeds:* Lady's bedstraw, meadow buttercup, corn chamomile, wild clary, cowslip, cranesbill, ox-eye daisy, foxglove, harebell, corn marigold, field scabious, teasel, toadflax.

Growing your own – a millionaire for a few pence

Trying to tame nature's fickleness is all part of the thrill of gardening. As much as the tending and nurturing of green things, it's our opportunity to create a dream view of the world. I'm with the mid-20th-century domestic goddess Constance Spry, who in her classic book *Simple Flowers – A Millionaire for a Few Pence* finds floral riches in a simple packet of seeds. How wonderful it would be if she could float down from the great garden in the sky and persuade all the teenage daughters in the land to give up dreams of Prada handbags, and get a longer lasting natural fix with a couple of quid spent on pots of nodding marigolds.

Even if the garden is a window box on a sill or a cluster of potted plants, it is so filled with the possibilities of pleasure. I cycle through bland Brixton estates and see optimistic hanging balcony gardens of Babylon, from a Bengali family's trailing beans and gourds to a hotchpotch of olive oil tins planted with tomatoes and mint belonging to a Greek contemplating tasty salads to serve with his grilled meat.

The serendipity of gardening also means you can do all the wrong things to a plant, and yet be surprised by a positive outcome, such as the desiccated lavender cutting I forgot all about that's now luxuriant and bushy, or bulbs planted at the last minute in January that still come up. Equally you can fuss and fret over your crop of prize tomatoes, but can't prevent some nasty black spot rot that destroys the lot.

Not everyone has the time or inclination to tend vegetables or any plant from seed, because, like looking after small children or a cat or a dog, it's rewarding, but requires effort. It is good, therefore, that there is the option of buying young plants to put straight into the ground or a container.

I always invest in some back-up plants in case of a seed disaster, especially the bean crop, which I would miss very much. The good sources are community allotments and plant stalls in markets. My tomatoes and French beans usually come from the local all-purpose hardware shop in the high street.

Spring greens and other seasonal vegetables

'The English have but three vegetables and two of them are cabbage.' Walter Hines Page, American ambassador to the Court of St James's

We have been through a bad patch in the kitchen ... for about the last couple of hundred years. But now? In our food enlightened culture, where cooking lessons have returned to school and fresh sweet green shoots and roots are everywhere,

slimy cabbage boiled and stirred to green rags – which my great grandmother was brilliant at – would be dumped in the (recycling) bin. Modern children are even being persuaded to eat up their greens when fresh and cooked with the new lightness of touch.

I wouldn't go so far as to say that I could live on cabbage, as it gets really tedious having the same food over and over – but if it were to be the season's very sweet and succulent spring greens, then let's say it wouldn't be a bad thing to have a daily plateful. These loose-leafed green cabbages without hearts need only a few seconds in boiling water. Use only their jade inner leaves; the bitter, dark green outer leaves should be ruthlessly stripped away. Alternatively, quickly stir fry them with garlic, or add to stews or hearty soups at the last moment. Spring greens are often sold with their mud, which all adds to the experience.

If you intend to be as ruthless as I suggest, buy about double the amount you think you will need. You can wash and strip the leaves down once home, then lightly dry and store them in the salad box of the refrigerator until needed.

Purple sprouting broccoli

I'm very sniffy about supermarket packed fruit and veg – don't you hate all that plastic packaging? But I'll make an exception for bobbly-headed spears of purple sprouting broccoli, which for some reason this year have been tricky to come by in the local greengrocer. And when I have found some they are quite often tired, floppy and dog-eared. The supermarket specimens, though, have been a triumph, but I will endeavour next year to pedal over to the farmers' market at my son's old school, where I know there won't be a limp leaf or plastic packet in sight.

Purple sprouting broccoli is in season roughly from January to May and, as with spring greens, is full of vitamin C, iron and fibre. When it is really fresh from picking, the spears snap cleanly. Other than picking off a few old leaves, the whole spear is edible. Try bunching them together with a band or piece of string and steam them standing up in the pan with the lid on for 10 minutes or so, as you might with asparagus, so that the flower buds don't overcook. Drain and eat as an exquisite spring lunch or supper dish with dollops of hollandaise (see left, and page 99 for the hollandaise recipe). The spears are also delicious tossed in melted butter, lemon and garlic, or served with a poached egg on top.

Runner beans

The more richly composted the soil, the bigger the crop, which is why grandma was able to send great, lumpy, paper-wrapped parcels of her runner bean glut every summer. Seaweed was the magic nourishment and, from when he was small, my father was given the task of carting slopping bucketfuls from the beach. It was then dug into a trench, which in the spirit of wartime economy was lined with newspaper to conserve moisture.

As with French beans, don't sow runners outside until May, and give them plenty of room and long canes for support. Plant 5cm (2 inches) deep and don't water them until they have germinated.

French beans

(see left for seed collected from last year's crop)

French beans are ideal for patio containers as well as flower beds. Make wigwams with canes or willow sticks for them to climb up. Try Fasold, stringless mid-green pods with mauve flowers.

Top and tail and eat lightly steamed with garlic, melted butter and lemon, or toss into a simple Salade Niçoise (see page 91).

Courgettes

Courgettes require sun and space, but aren't otherwise a bother to grow. Sow April to June, 5cm (2 inches) deep, 90cm (36 inches) apart, or start off in pots. Plant out hardened-off seedlings after the risk of frost. Set beer traps because the young tender leaves are as attractive to slugs as chocolate biscuits are to a serial dieter.

Most grow as bushes, but there are useful trailing varieties. Try Tromboncino and Black Forest, which can be trained up supports or over archways. Courgettes take about eight weeks to mature, and be vigilant once the young fruits start to develop, as they can grow to harvest size within a couple of days and quickly become marrows. Pick them regularly and they'll crop for most of the season. One plant will yield about 20 courgettes.

Griddled slices of courgette with olive oil and lemon and garlic are delicious; so too are the flowers, which can be fried in a beer batter.

Swiss chard

Easy to grow, Swiss chard needs well-nourished soil and water and takes about two months to mature. It's worth buying as small plants because you only need a few for a good supply. It produces spinach-like leaves and vibrant coloured stems from June into winter. It is much hardier than spinach in the heat. I like the painterly pinks and yellows of the 'Rainbow Mixed' variety. I eat the stems and young leaves lightly steamed and tossed with toasted pine nuts, olive oil and lemon juice.

Potatoes

The art of chitting
'Chitting' potatoes means encouraging the seed potatoes to sprout before planting. You want the shoots or 'eyes' to be firm and holding the nutrients before they go into the ground. If left in too dark or too warm a place, the tubers will sprout too early and produce weak and pale leggy sprouts.

Get your seed potatoes early in the spring, and 'chit' them by standing them on end in trays or boxes, with the 'rose' end uppermost, i.e. the end that contains the most 'eyes'. Put them on a shelf but not in a warm room. So long as they are not frozen it is much better to keep them cool.

By planting time, potato tubers will have produced strong little green shoots, which will enable them to start growing as soon as they are planted. Plant them from March to May, as soon as the risk of frost has passed, 10–13cm (4–5 inches) deep in shallow ridges 20–30cm (8–12 inches) apart, with 60cm (24 inches) between each row.

Not the best vegetable to grow in small spaces, but there's something truly exciting, especially for children, about experiencing earthy and freshly dug spuds, rather than those brought home in a plastic bag from the supermarket.

Just to enjoy the potato experience, I recommend growing a couple of rows of, say, Pink Fir Apple, for salads.

Peas

Sow peas from March onwards, and you could be eating sweet, tender peas straight from the pod all through the summer months. Prepare a planting site by digging over your plot and adding compost or well-rotted manure.

Make sure the ground is warm and dry before sowing. Sow seeds in a flat trench, 5cm (2 inches) deep and 25cm (10 inches) wide. Water the trench first, then sow the seeds 5–7cm (2–3 inches) apart in three rows along the trench.

Peas are climbers and many old varieties reach heights of 200cm (6–7ft). Put supports in place before young plants become top-heavy. Regular picking is essential for a truly fresh pea.

Harvest from the bottom of the plant, working upwards. Do not pull the plant after harvesting, as the roots are full of nitrogen-fixing bacteria. Cut off the stems at ground level and allow the roots to rot down.

Radishes

These crunchy, peppery roots look as if a French Impressionist has got at them and dipped their skins in pink, leaving little white tips. They are very fast to grow from seed; try baguette-shaped French Breakfast. Sow from February to September. Keep moist and thin as necessary. Repeat sowings every two to three weeks to ensure a continuous crop throughout the summer.

It's much more economical to sow little and often than to have a long row of radishes coming to maturity at the same time. They can also be grown as a 'catch crop' between slower growing vegetables.

A bowl of radishes and a dish of sea salt to dip them in is a simple summer still life – as good to eat as it is to look at (see pages 156–57).

Tomatoes

In our unreliable climate I find it more rewarding to grow smaller cherry varieties of tomatoes. Try Gardener's Delight or Sweet Million – these seem to ripen more effectively and are sweeter than larger varieties, which in a dismal summer often don't get past the green stage and are fit only for chutney. This year I am feeding the tomatoes with my sister-in-law's homemade comfrey fertilizer*, so they should be good. For some simple recipes with tomatoes see page 78.

*If you have a small patch of comfrey leaves, collect them and put them in a bucket of water and leave to soak for up to a month. Drain off the liquid and use dilluted in 1 to 10 parts water. It stinks but is a wonderful food for all vegetables.

Leeks

I don't bother to grow onions, they're quite labour intensive, and so cheap and widely available that it's not worth the trouble. Sweet young leeks are another thing. They can either be sown in a seedbed in spring for transplanting the following summer, or sown in their permanent positions. Try Lyon, an autumn variety with mild-tasting long stems, or Musselburgh, a winter-hardy leek with white stems.

Sow thinly about 2.5cm (1 inch) apart in drills about 0.5cm (¼ inch) deep and cover with finely sifted soil. If you sow in a seed bed you have the added bother of transplanting; on the other hand, if they are sown in their permanent position they will take up a lot of space for a long time before producing results. Plant seedlings out in May or June. Harvest from mid-autumn through to the end of late spring, depending on the time of sowing and the variety.

Steam leeks, sauté in butter, or add to soups (see page 17 for Wild garlic soup).

Shallots

I won't say no to growing shallots – small but perfectly formed onions that are so useful for roasting or throwing in a stew. They take up less space than onions, and grown this year for the first time have proved very easy. The bulbs are planted in rows in February and March, by just pressing them into the soil, so that they are about half buried. Beyond keeping them free of weeds, no further attention is required until July, when they should be pulled and laid in the sun to ripen thoroughly. Lift and plant as you would garlic.

Garlic

Garlic and other members of the onion family are good companion plants to help deter greenfly and other pests.

Ideal for the smallest of spaces and a doddle to grow. You can use plump heads from the greengrocer, but a grower will sell different varieties such as Arno or Solent Wight. Plant in spring or autumn for harvesting in August or June respectively. Break the bulb into individual cloves, and push into the soil 5cm (2 inches) deep, 15cm (6 inches) apart. Water well in prolonged dry spells and the garlic is ready to lift when the tops turn yellow and start to dry out. Lift out with a fork, shake off the excess soil from the hairy roots, and dry by hanging inside or out in a sheltered spot. Plait into braided lengths and store somewhere cool. Save some of the fattest cloves to plant next year.

I like to roast whole bulbs, cut in half around the middle as they look very pretty and botanical this way.

Garlicky alioli mayonnaise (see page 101) is one of my summer staples, easy to make and delicious with everything from raw vegetables to grilled fish and meat.

Sowing seeds

'The love of gardening is a seed that once sown never dies.' Gertrude Jekyll

I tend to pick up seed packets on a whim rather than on a preordained expedition. I know more or less what I want, but like to gather together elements of my summer garden bit by bit. It gives me breathing space to mull over ideas. It's not that I'm a procrastinator, rather that I enjoy the adventure of coming across surprises, like the chilli seeds raised by Latin American chilli lovers at the local community allotments.

When I was visiting my father in Somerset, I wandered into a typical country high-street hardware shop brimming with tools and, inspired by the equally well stocked racks of seeds, bought packets of zinnias – the colours were so irresistible. And at the local deli-cum-café-cum-veg shop, summer visions of salads tumbled with leaves of aromatic basil meant there was no alternative but to ditch smelly cheese for two varieties of basil from the artfully packed range of Italian Franchi seeds.

The sprouting seed trays lined up in my office, like cots in a nursery, get under my feet as the fledging plants make their break towards the light. Time to transplant the zinnias into peat pots, which can go straight into the ground later on, as they don't do well with too much handling of the roots. I have a passion for the riotous pinks and purples of this frilly late-summer flower, which looks so colourful in the border and as decoration.

Successful seed germination depends on moisture, warmth, air and eventually light. Generally seeds should be sown to a depth equal to their thickness, though

fleshy seeds such as runner beans should be sown 5cm (2 inches) deep. Small seeds require only a very fine soil covering, and dust-like seeds, especially if sown under glass, need no other covering than a pane of glass and a sheet of brown paper.

Some seeds are hardy and can be planted straight out where they flower, while others are semi-hardy and need to be started off and protected from frost in a greenhouse or cold frame before they are planted out in April or May.

Even if you don't have either of these, it is still possible to make a mini greenhouse by doing inventive things such as cutting a 2-litre (3½-pint) plastic bottle in half, placing the top half over your pot of newly planted seeds, and putting it on a sunny windowsill.

Growing seeds in pots

Starting seeds in pots requires decent seed compost and a container, which could be anything from a cardboard egg tray to a used ice-cream box.

As a rule of thumb, sow larger seeds such as sweet peas in threes to a pot, versus a good scattering of pinprick-sized seeds of plants such as nicotiana (tobacco plant), basil or stocks. Move them out of direct sunlight as this will make the seedling stems develop quicker than their roots.

Keep the compost moist, watering every two to three days. It must not dry out. Once the seedlings have four leaves, the strongest ones can be pricked out very gently with a fork or teaspoon. Move into modules – one plant per little pot – or into small pots 6–9cm (2½–3½ inches) wide. Make a hole with a pencil, and sink the plant into it; the seed leaves should almost rest on the compost. Firm them in carefully so that their roots are not left in air pockets.

Planting seedlings into the ground or larger pots

First water the fledgling plants (about 12.5cm/6 inches high). With a trowel, dig a hole large enough to take the root ball easily – none of the root ball must be proud of the earth after planting. Put one hand over the top of the pot with a finger gently on either side of the plant's stem to hold it in, turn it upside down, and lift the pot off. Once the plant is in the soil, firm the soil gently around it. Water well.

You can use any container for a patio or window ledge as long as it has enough holes in the bottom for good drainage. Galvanised metal buckets look utilitarian but stylish, and terracotta is good. You can give shiny plastic tubs a smarter look by sanding them and giving them a wash of emulsion in white or bean green.

Sowing directly into the ground

Sow seeds directly into the ground with a shaking action straight from the packet, or with pinches of seed picked from the palm of the hand. Before you sow, dig the soil as deeply as possible and mix in some compost, but dig it in at least 15cm (6 inches) below the surface. Seedlings grow better without compost until they have built up a good digestive system; by that time, the roots will find the manure down below and make good use of it.

Make a short drill by pressing the handle of a rake or hoe into the soil surface, or scratch the furrow with the pointed end of a plant label. For longer drills, stretch garden twine tight between two pegs as a guide. Firm the soil gently over the seeds with the back of a hoe or rake, or by treading lightly to help preserve moisture around the seeds and assist germination.

Keep down weeds by frequent hoeing as soon as the rows of seedlings appear. Thin out the seedlings when they have two or three leaves so that they have sufficient space to develop laterally and make bushy growth.

Some useful garden kit

A weathered, galvanized metal watering can looks more at home in the garden than a bright plastic one, although the latter is lighter to handle. Look in junk shops for a lovely old grey metal shape with a long spout and a nice wide rose head.

A rake with 10 or 12 teeth is handy for levelling soil and preparing seed beds. Fan-shaped lawn rakes with springy wire prongs are good for removing moss and dead grass.

I keep a pair of secateurs in my apron pocket when I'm out and about in the garden. You never know when you want to deadhead a rose or snip a dead branch.

A trowel is the best tool for planting small plants and bulbs. Some trowel blades are graduated as a guide to planting depths.

Garden forks are essential for digging and breaking up the soil. Hand forks, often sold in sets with trowels, are really useful for weeding.

Spades are invaluable for many tasks, from turning the vegetable patch over in winter to digging a trench for beans. Stainless steel spades are the most expensive but won't corrode.

The compost bucket

I have been wielding the fork and spade to prepare my vegetable patch, turning the soil over and over to break it up. One irritating aspect is that the cat and dog think I'm doing this for their benefit – creating a new and soft litter tray. My deterrent against the pets and the squirrels is some fine netting. I really feel like an old-time gardener as I dig in bucketfuls of home-grown kitchen compost.

The compost starts life in the old metal bucket by the back door, which contains forensic detail of the family's eating habits – coffee grounds, old tea bags (Earl Grey, mint, lemon and ginger), piles of potato peelings (must be Sunday lunch), overripe bananas (no one eats them if so much as a black tinge appears on the skin), apple cores and eggshells. When it's full the contents are chucked in the plastic domed compost bin supplied by the council.

The edible peelings are joined by grass cuttings, dead flowers, leaves, loo roll tubes and cardboard. As practised by all proper composters, cooked food (even vegetable waste) is blacklisted: it attracts vermin. Citrus peel is supposed to be too acidic but I sneak it in and it doesn't seem to be a problem.

I can't say that I do enough turning and titivating of my compost, but I do manage each spring to shovel good, dark, earthy and organic-smelling material from the bottom layers of the bin. Like coins in a Christmas pudding, foreign objects often emerge, too: rusty knives, that silver teaspoon I thought was lost and even a false nail.

Worms
Earthworms help aerate
the soil and improve
soil fertility by carrying
organic matter
underground.

I use a single bin – or you can use a heap with no bin at all. But if you've got the space, the ideal compost heap is divided into three compartments in wooden slatted bins; the first section is for fresh waste, the second is for moving the contents of the first compartment into, and the third is for storing the mature compost in.

A simple way to make compost

Start with a layer of straw or twigs to allow the air to circulate. Add a layer of grass cuttings and weeds. Add the contents of the kitchen bucket, plus water if the heap gets too dry.

Once a week or so, turn the heap with a fork, boosting the nitrogen content with natural activators such as grass cuttings and animal manure (not from the family cat or dog or battery-reared chickens).

To speed up the rotting process and keep the pile warm and covered from rain, use wood or a bit of wool carpet or coir.

A SIMPLE VALENTINE

'In the Spring a young man's fancy lightly turns to thoughts of love.'
Alfred Lord Tennyson

Love is in the air. Woo your intended with a DIY heart-shaped token. More meaningful and more creative than anything shop-bought, it can be as elaborate or as simple as you please.

felt, fabric, or tissue paper (see what you can find around the house – you could even use the back of an old envelope or carrier bag)
a heart stencil to get the shape (a heart biscuit cutter for example, or, if you feel confident enough, draw it freehand on paper and cut it out)
scissors
all-purpose glue – without solvents if possible
plain paper or card
enough ribbon to fold into a bow

Outline the heart shape on your piece of fabric, paper, or whatever you choose, by drawing around the cookie cutter or paper heart stencil. Cut it out. Apply two or three blobs of glue and stick it in place on the piece of plain paper or card. Fold the ribbon into a bow; apply a little bit of glue to the top of the heart and stick the bow onto it.

Make your effort more seductive and scent the paper with a few drops of rose or lavender water. Write your heart's desires on the back or front of the card and send it immediately.

By the way, if you are on holiday in Spain, chemists there do very good inexpensive colognes because the Spanish are fond of smelling delicious during their evening *paseos*. Wrap up a bottle for your suitcase.

BREAKFAST

**Good things for
breakfast in bed:**

Homemade marmalade
(see page 260)

Grilled field mushrooms
on toast (see page 164)

Champagne and fresh
orange juice

Mint tea
Place a sprig of mint in
a glass and pour boiling
water over it. Leave to
infuse for a few minutes.

Crumbs and the caramel taste of toast are good breakfast-in-bed companions. So too is thick coffee from a screwtop espresso pot. The satisfaction factor of a cup of coffee depends so much on how it is served: vast mugs don't work for me compared to the neater handling of a small chunky white cup and saucer. Arrange it all on a tray. My grandmother was expert: white cloth, folded white napkin, slab of butter, not too hard, not too soft, and toast in a rack, crusts off, all making its way regally on the Stannah stairlift to her mother, and my great-grandmother of the overcooked cabbage fame.

I use a rather groovy, white plastic tray with metal legs – the whole affair is more balanced, more secure. I wouldn't recommend a round tray so much as a rectangular one with high-ish sides to stop things sliding off. You could also give a new look to an old tray with a couple of coats of retro-style duck egg blue paint.

Flapping sheets on the washing line

Beat the moth
Lavender, cloves,
cinnamon, black pepper
and orris root in a
muslin bag will deter
moths from destroying
your best wool blankets.
Cedar wood balls are
also good moth
deterrents.

The people who come to use our house as a location for lifestyle catalogue shoots do not want real-life jam stains, dog hairs and muddy paw prints spoiling their 'new look' for whatever season they happen to be promoting. (In spring, actually, everyone is working on the following winter.) I am therefore frequently stripping the beds and filling up the washing machine with a white tangle of sheets and pillowcases. Apart from washing at lower temperatures to save energy, I also use half the detergent suggested, and one that is an eco product.

Blankets
Wash blankets on a wool cycle with a gentle detergent. If there is no machine, wash in the bath and tread with bare feet. Rinse in several changes of water and squeeze out any excess. Dry flat over a collapsible airer or between two chairs out in the garden.

Here are some ways to look after bedlinen: Soak stains in hot soapy water before laundering. Don't hang sheets out in a gale or they may be whipped into holes if they're wearing thin. I'm not suggesting you should be a domestic paragon and iron the bed linen, but if you have the inclination or time, iron pure linen while it is damp; the heavier the linen, the damper it should be for ironing. For both cotton and linen textures, fold sheets and pillowcases flat as they're taken off the line. Iron pillowcases from the edge inwards. Fold sheets evenly and press the creases in by hand. Folds should not be ironed into bedlinen, so the experts say. If bedlinen has yellowed after being stored, rewash and dry it in sunlight, which has wonderful whitening qualities. This feature is obviously not so good if you want to preserve the colour in a fabric, in which case dry out of direct sunlight.

A GOOD EGG

Egg magic
Eggs often play the part of the magic ingredient in the kitchen. They are used to create emulsions such as mayonnaise, alioli and hollandaise sauce; an egg wash will turn pastry a golden colour, and beaten egg white provides the fluffy body for a soufflé or meringue.

Along with all the greenness of spring there's the perfect simplicity of another symbol of renewal: the humble egg. Years ago you could take your pick. Lapwings were so common that people wolfed down their eggs and still the population soared. Or how about a tasty boiled plover's egg? In *Brideshead Revisited*, Evelyn Waugh's teddy-bear-carrying Sebastian gives them to his guests.'

Though far too many eggs from horrible battery farms come to the contemporary table, the tale is not all doom and gloom. Like many townies who've escaped to the country, my horse-and dog-mad sister keeps giddy hens who sometimes peck at her choice plants, but in return lay a daily batch of golden yolks, the eggs all warm and stuck with straw. (This picture of bucolic romance, by the way, is interrupted at least once a year when the fox tears them apart and she has to start all over again.)

And then there's the way that, when it isn't focused on trivia, TV can be really positive for good eggs such as chef Jamie Oliver, whose programmes have forced egg producers to sharpen up their act. At least the better supermarkets now supply organic eggs that are free-range and chemical- and antibiotic-free. I guess that in every area of food production, the only way we can be sure about the integrity of our eggs is if we know where they've come from. So it isn't surprising that on a breezy morning at the Saturday market in Olhão, Portugal, when I point at the blue plastic washing-up bowl filled with gleaming white eggs and the weathered stallholder says '*minhas galinhas*' (my hens), I come away with the lot.

Eggs are the ultimate fast food. Even if the cupboard is almost Mother Hubbard bare, a dozen eggs on standby can be made into an array of breakfast ideas. It takes less than five minutes to whisk up scrambled eggs and smoked salmon – a treat in our house on Sundays and holidays – or to hard boil a dozen tiny speckled quails' eggs (3 minutes) to peel and dip in salt and black pepper. (This is also a useful way to encourage pernickety children to eat up their eggs – minus the salt and pepper.) How about poached eggs or eggy bread for the morning after the night before? Or there is the possibility of a more exotic egg adventure such as Middle Eastern hamine eggs, which are whole eggs simmered overnight with oil and onions, so that the flavour permeates right through.

Free-range or organic?

Note that not all free-range eggs are organic and deep yellow yolks can be created by artificial colouring in the feed. Organic yolks are likely to be paler due to the lack of colourings in the bird's diet.

Boiled eggs

Cooking times:

2–3 minutes: soft with a runny yolk and white

5–6 minutes: firm white, soft yolk

10 minutes: hard-boiled

Some people crack the top with a small spoon and peel the shell, or maybe you're someone who slices it off cleanly with a knife. However you open a boiled egg, it is obligatory to eat it with buttered toast. Cut same toast into thin soldiers (crusts off) for children to dip in their morning egg.

Fine-tuning the consistency comes, of course, with practice. I was brought up with the 'four-minute egg' – anything more and my father would complain that it was hard; anything less and it was too runny. This was yet another area in which I had to put up with the unreasonableness of adults, but at least I had fun watching the grains of sand run through the egg timer.

Bring a saucepan of water to the boil and slide in the egg on a spoon. Room temperature eggs are less likely to crack than very cold ones.

Fried eggs with sage

I came across this idea – an alternative to the normal 'greasy spoon' breakfast – at Leila's café in Shoreditch, east London, where trendy art students wolf down hearty and inventive plates of home-cooked fare.

2 tbsp unsalted butter
handful of chopped sage
4 eggs
sea salt and freshly ground black pepper

Melt the butter in a frying pan, add the sage and cook until crispy on a medium heat. Remove the sage and put to one side. Crack the eggs into the same pan and cook until the yolks are firm. Season to taste and serve garnished with the sage.

Scrambled eggs

Scrambled eggs are always soothing; pale yellow eggy mounds served plain with salt and pepper, or dressed up with everything from grated Parmesan to a handful of chopped chives.

Melt a large lump of unsalted butter in a heavy-based saucepan to stop the eggs sticking and add as many beaten eggs as you need (about 2 per person). Cook on a low heat and stir continuously with a wooden spoon until creamy, no more than a few minutes. Do not stop to put the washing out.

Take off the heat just before the egg mixture is set, as it will carry on cooking quite quickly with its own heat and that of the pan.

Stir in any of the following: Chopped anchovies; skinned and chopped roasted tomato and chopped basil (great colours); chopped smoked salmon and dill (also good to look at); chopped steamed asparagus (as in *revueltos huevos*, which the Spanish eat in spring with gangly wild asparagus, *espárragos trigueros*); chopped tarragon, chives or marjoram (nice and herby, good green colours, too).

A word of warning
Remember to put the pan in to soak immediately. Cooked egg is one of the worst things to remove (along with baked-on porridge) if left to go cold.

Omelette

For a Spanish version, see how to make a tortilla on page 104.

Whenever I've not got a clue what to cook for dinner, an omelette – along with anything on a pasta theme – is unlikely to be spurned by my children. It cooks so fast, only a minute or so, so it is no chore to make separate ones for everyone around the table. I usually serve omelettes with a green salad.

Beat 2 or 3 eggs together in a bowl and season (add chopped herbs or grated cheese if you like).

Heat a frying pan with a knob of unsalted butter. I suggest a pan 15cm (6 inches) in diameter – any smaller, the omelette will be too thick, and any larger too thin.

Pour the eggs into the pan, spreading the mixture evenly. After a few seconds tilt the pan to and fro, and using a wooden spoon push the edges of the forming omelette into the centre, letting the uncooked egg run into the space.

When there's only a bit of runniness left on the top, either fold the omelette in half or bring both edges into the middle, placing one edge on top of the other.

Serve immediately. An omelette is better undercooked than overcooked.

Pancakes

serves 4 (2 each)

Pancakes are a delicious and utilitarian food, great for stuffing with refrigerator leftovers: chopped cooked chicken, spring onions, and a squeeze of lemon bound together with fromage frais is a tasty lunch/ snack idea.

Waffle, bao bing, blini, drop scone, crêpe: a world tour in pancakes. I remember crunching sand with the butter and sugar stickiness of the lacy crêpes sold on the beach in 1960s' Bordeaux. Another summer, in Sweden (naked plunges in icy lakes, surreal daylight at 2am), we mopped up piles of Mrs Lanstrom's pancakes stuffed with whipped cream and juicy lingonberries.

Tossing pancakes on Shrove Tuesday, the last day before Lent, is never missed in our house.

100g/3½oz/scant ¾ cup plain flour
½ tsp sea salt
l egg, beaten
250ml/8fl oz/1 cup milk
2 tbsp unsalted butter

Put the flour and salt in a bowl. Make a well and pour in the egg and milk. Stir well with a wooden spoon until the batter is smooth. Add a little more milk if necessary. Leave to stand for half an hour.

Heat the butter in a small, nonstick frying pan. When it is very hot, add about 2 tablespoons of the batter – enough to coat the bottom of the pan. Tilt so that it spreads evenly. Cook for about a minute until bubbles appear and the bottom is golden brown. Turn the pancake with a spatula or toss it, and cook the other side.

Sprinkle with caster sugar and juice squeezed from an orange or lemon wedge and roll up each pancake. Eat immediately.

FROM EGGS TO EASTER

Like secret jewels nestling in the grass, under a cup or on the corner of a window sill, solid chocolate eggs wrapped in shiny pink, gold, green and blue foil are worthy treasures in the breathless rush and furious clue-solving of an Easter egg hunt. The best ones are made by Lindt, available in good sweet shops around Easter time. We used to have them as children and I would hoard my stash under the pillow and eat them at night, leaving telltale chocolate smears and bits of silvery paper on the sheets. Along with the egg hunt, we decorated eggs to put in a bowl at the centre of the table.

Painted eggs

This is an exercise with little waste, because the contents of blown eggs will make a very tasty tortilla (see page 104).

white or blue duck eggs, blown (see method)
pin
pencil
art masking fluid
acrylic paint – greens and pinks are spring-like
paintbrush

To blow the egg, make a hole with a pin in each end of the egg, and blow the yolk and white into a bowl. This may require some huffing and puffing if the hole is too small. Wash and dry the egg. Gently push the tip of a pencil through one of the holes in the egg to support it while decorating. Use the art masking fluid to paint your pattern on the egg; spots, stripes, zigzags, anything you like. Leave it to dry.

When it's dry, mix the acrylic paint with a little water and paint over the egg, including the masked areas. Leave the egg to dry for about 20 minutes, then gently rub the masked areas with your fingertip – the painted latex will pull off easily to reveal the pattern, which will be the white or blue of the shell, contrasting with the painted colour.

This is very simple, and has a lovely naive quality. Pile the eggs onto a plate for decoration at the Easter table or give as a gift instead of the chocolate variety.

Flower fairies

Improvisation is the key to imaginative and cut-price fancy dress outfits, from a Halloween cat (black tights, crayoned whiskers and a long tail made from a taped-up bin bag) to a World War II evacuee (my old Fair Isle jumper, some long socks and pigtails).

But there are times when I want to eat my words, such as realizing two hours before the event that I have completely forgotten to organize flower fairy party kits for my two girls. Keep cool, breathe deeply, count to ten: you are running in the never-ending race to be a good mother.

Somehow the craft neurons are activated and I grab a length of printed white voile used on a shoot, cut a rectangle, fold it in half and cut a small hole for the head. Da daah!! An instant flower fairy tunic, belted at the middle with a piece of ribbon. I raid daffodils in my mum's garden and wind them around a piece of wire, securing with tape. An instant flower fairy headdress.

As I scrape across the metaphorical finishing line, I think, 'Where's that very large glass of wine?'

Hot cross buns

makes a dozen or so buns

Racing to unfold twists of paper with handwritten clues to the stash of chocolate eggs was an Easter highlight. So too were the sticky and aromatic hot cross buns that appeared at breakfast on Good Friday. My mum bought them in white paper bags from the baker across the common and they were plump, sweet and bursting with currants. The 'two for one' packets of buns heaped by the checkout counter don't quite do it for me today, and so making our own is a good way to reclaim the pleasure.

450g/14½oz/3¼ cups plain flour
55g/2¼oz/generous ¼ cup caster sugar
pinch of mixed spice
1½ tsp dried yeast
75g/3oz/⅓ cup raisins
55g/2¼oz/¾ cup candied peel
grated rind of 1 orange
1 egg
1 tbsp milk
55g/2¼oz/½ stick unsalted butter, melted

Christians and pagans

The cross on the buns is said to be a symbol of the crucifixion; it may have more ancient origins too, with buns eaten in honour of the goddess Eostre (the origin of Easter) and marked with what might have been the four quarters of the moon, or the seasons.

for the cross
80g/3oz/generous ½ cup plain flour
2 tbsp caster sugar
100ml/3½fl oz/½ cup water

for the glaze
2 tbsp soft brown sugar
2 tbsp milk
1 tbsp marmalade

Sift the flour into a bowl and add the sugar, mixed spice, dried yeast, raisins, candied peel and grated orange rind. Beat the egg with the milk and add the melted butter. Tip the mixture into the flour and stir. Turn out and knead on a floured surface for 5 minutes. Divide into 12 buns and place on floured baking sheets. Cover with a damp tea towel. Leave in a warm place for about 90 minutes, until doubled in size.

To make the cross: Mix the flour, sugar and water until smooth. Put the mixture in a piping bag or a plastic freezer bag with one corner snipped off and pipe a cross onto each bun. Place in a preheated oven, 180°C/350°F/Gas Mark 4, for 20 minutes. Cool on a wire rack.

To make the glaze: Simmer the sugar, milk and marmalade in a pan for a few minutes until syrupy, stirring all the time. Sieve the syrup to remove any pieces of orange rind and pour over the cooked buns.

A SPRING FEAST

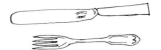

Sunday lunch. Sweet mint, rosemary and roasting smells from the oven, and it's just warm enough to open the window and let in air lightly scented with the witch-hazel flowers from next door's garden. I like to serve up on the sort of white oval china platter that used to be staple in old-fashioned kitchens. On a hunt around the charity shop last week I added to my collection with a couple of generous shapes, a little worn, but this adds to their appeal. These, together with flowers and a white cloth, are simple ideas to create a sense of occasion.

To roast a leg of lamb

serves 4–6

Rub the skin of a 1.5–2kg/3–4lb leg of lamb with sea salt and freshly ground black pepper. Make 15 or so small incisions with a sharp knife and insert slivers of garlic and small sprigs of rosemary. All of this will permeate to make the meat taste gloriously garlicky and aromatic.

Transfer the lamb to a roasting tin and place in a preheated oven, 190°C/375°F/Gas Mark 5, for about 1½ hours, turning over once, for a pinkish inside. At the end of the cooking time, remove the lamb from the oven and leave it to rest in the roasting tin for 10–15 minutes, covered with foil or a clean tea towel to keep it warm. Serve garnished with generous sprigs of fresh rosemary.

For a more intense flavour, rub 3 or 4 salted anchovies into the flesh along with the rosemary and garlic.

Simple gravy

Georgie, my middle daughter, is chief gravy-maker, partly because she's very good at it, but partly because she gets to help herself as 'cook's perks' to the largest serving. This is her recipe.

Heat a heavy-based frying pan on the hob. When hot, pour the juices from the roasting tin into the pan, and add glugs of red wine and Noilly Prat (not essential, but nice), 500ml/17fl oz/2 cups vegetable stock, a rosemary sprig and garlic and simmer until it starts to thicken, stirring constantly. If necessary, add a little sifted flour to thicken. When it's to your liking, season with salt and pepper to taste and strain into a jug.

Mint sauce

Mint sauce is a traditional lamb accompaniment but I also like to eat it with anything from grilled chicken to roast vegetables.

Chop the leaves finely from a generous handful of mint. Place the mint in a bowl and add a pinch of sea salt, 1 tablespoon of caster sugar and 4 tablespoons of boiling water. Stir and leave to cool, then add 4 tablespoons of cider vinegar, or more if you want the flavour to be sharper.

Spring greens

Serve lightly steamed with lemon, butter and garlic.

Roasted Jerusalem artichokes

Wash a kilo (2lb) of these knobbly roots with their fresh-from-the-earth flavour. Cut off all the fibrous extras, but don't peel (they're more robust and flavoursome with skins on).

Slice the Jerusalem artichokes into 1cm (½ inch) rounds, transfer to a roasting tin with olive oil, sea salt and pepper, and place in a preheated oven, 190°C/375°F/Gas Mark 5, for about 45 minutes. You can cook them in the same oven as the lamb, but start them off 15 minutes or so earlier, and move them to the lower rack when you put the lamb in. The main thing is not to let them overcook and become too dry and crispy.

Spring rack of lamb with mint, rosemary and mustard

serves 4

This is a really simple Sunday lunch idea, with tender meat from the rib section of the beast. You can serve it with anything from roast potatoes and a salad to roast artichokes and spring greens. Try to buy the season's new lamb and allow about three small chops per person; two if the racks are larger, or more if you're particularly flush and have hefty appetites.

Lamb goes well with sweet jellies of redcurrant, quince or crab apple (see page 176) and also mint sauce.

If you're not a red wine lover, try a chilled white oaky Rioja with this.

lamb racks with 2 or 3 cutlets per person

for the paste
1 tbsp olive oil
2 tbsp wholegrain or Dijon mustard
1 tbsp chopped mint leaves
1 tbsp chopped rosemary leaves
3 garlic cloves, chopped
sea salt and freshly ground black pepper

Score the flesh of the racks with a sharp knife. Mix the olive oil, mustard, mint, rosemary and garlic to a thick paste and season with salt and pepper. Rub the mixture into the flesh. Cover and marinate in the refrigerator for anything from an hour to all day.

Put the lamb in a roasting tin, flesh side up, and place in a preheated oven, 190°C/375°F/Gas Mark 5, for 15–25 minutes depending on the size of the rack. I like mine pink in the middle to enjoy the sweetness and tenderness of the meat.

Remove from the oven, cover with foil and rest for 5 minutes before carving into cutlets and serving on warmed plates.

Rhubarb for a spring pudding

Rhubarb's famous laxative qualities are a simple result of the gut rejecting its unusually high level of oxalic acid. Only if you ate the leaves, which are high in this, would you be in real trouble, but it is the plant's rich pink stalks that are edible and delicious.

The practice of 'forcing' rhubarb (covering the plant to encourage it to produce pale, fibrous, succulent shoots) was discovered by accident at Chelsea Physic Garden in 1817, when crowns were covered over after a ditch was cleared.

First mentioned as a food in France in 1778, by 1861 – when Mrs Beeton published her *Book of Household Management* – rhubarb was being made into pies, jam and wine in most households, and the floppy great leaves stood in the corner of every vegetable plot. If you want to grow it, consider the following varieties: Valentine, Early Red, Glaskins Perpetual.

Baked rhubarb

Tart to taste and beautiful, a few sticks of rhubarb need little more than to be chopped into 2.5cm (1 inch) chunks after washing, put in a baking tray with several large spoons of soft brown sugar, a little orange rind and some grated ginger, and placed in a preheated oven, 180°C/350°F/Gas Mark 4, for 20 minutes or so, until slightly crunchy on the outside but soft inside.

Rhubarb crumble

serves 4–6

for the crumble
300g/10oz/generous 2 cups plain flour
175g/6oz/1 cup soft brown sugar
200g/7oz/1¾ sticks unsalted butter, cubed, at room temperature

for the filling
500g/1lb/3 cups rhubarb, cut into 2.5cm (1 inch) chunks
150g/5oz/¾ cup brown sugar
grated rind and juice of 1 small orange
grated rind and juice of 1 lemon

Mix the flour and sugar in a large bowl, then rub in the butter, a few cubes at a time, until the mixture resembles breadcrumbs.

Place the rhubarb, sugar and orange and lemon rind and juice in a 24cm (9½ inch) ovenproof dish. Spoon over the crumble mix. Bake in a preheated oven, 180°C/350°F/Gas Mark 4, for 40–45 minutes until the crumble is browned and the fruit mixture bubbling.

Serve with cream, ice cream, fromage frais and maybe, if you want to be more decadent, a glass of sweet muscatel wine.

Rhubarb fool

serves 4–6

Serve from the refrigerator in simple glasses with chunks of homemade shortbread (see page 68).

500g/1lb/3 cups rhubarb, cut into 2.5cm (1 inch) chunks
100g/3½ oz/½ cup caster sugar
grated rind and juice of 1 orange
250ml/8fl oz/generous 1 cup double cream

Put the rhubarb chunks in a pan with the sugar and the orange rind and juice. Cover and simmer gently for 10–15 minutes, stirring regularly. The rhubarb should be soft but not mushy.

Taste it and add more sugar if needed. Allow the rhubarb to cool completely. Whip the cream until it forms soft peaks. Fold the rhubarb mixture into the cream gently with a metal spoon so the cream doesn't lose its volume.

TIPTOE THROUGH THE TULIPS
AND OTHER SPRING BULBS

Bulb tips:

To create a really good display in a container, plant bulbs at different depths to fit more into the space.

Remove flower heads when they have faded, otherwise the plant will divert energy from building up the bulb, which is necessary for next year's display, and put it instead into seed production. Conversely, let the leaves die back and return nourishment to the bulb.

To make more of your snowdrops, divide any clumps after flowering but while still in leaf. Carefully fork up and prise apart the separate bulbs with their leaves, and replant them in drifts around shrubs and trees.

Thank goodness it's not 1637, when the 'Tulipomania' bubble burst in Holland, and tulip traders could no longer find new buyers willing to pay increasingly inflated prices for their bulbs. Like the sub-prime mortgage debacle in the US, the demand for tulips collapsed and prices plummeted from the dizzy heights of exchanging 5 hectares (12 acres) of land for a couple of 'Semper Augustus' bulbs. Read *The Tulip₃* by Anna Pavord, which details the rise of tulips as must-have luxury items and status symbols.

Like a hierarchy of designer handbags, they were classified in groups; single-coloured tulips of red, yellow or white were known as Couleren, but it was the multi-coloured that were the most popular. Red or pink on a white background were christened Rosen; purple or lilac on a white background were called Violetten; and red, brown or purple on a yellow background were known as Bizarden. These highly sought-after tulip bulbs produced flowers in vivid colours, shot through with lines and flame shapes, which are now known to be due to the 'Tulip breaking virus'.

Tulips should be planted in November, about 10cm (4 inches) deep, and may be left in the ground for several years, but it is worth lifting the bulbs and replanting them annually. My favourites are the fimbriated Parrot varieties, which I buy at happily uninflated prices online. I plant them sparingly in each bed (see pages 26–27) – I think they look more beautiful this way.

I'm really pleased that the black Parrot tulips from last season have reappeared. It is absorbing to watch them bud and unfurl into a whirl of feathery petals the deep colour of beetroot. Unfurled 'blue' Parrot tulips look like striped fruit drops from an old-fashioned confectioner or even a head of salad radicchio. When they are in full bloom (see previous page), the striped effect fades into an all-over fuchsia pink. New to my garden this year is the single late tulip Violet Beauty, in rich fuchsia pink, a slender, more elegant thing than its wayward and feathery Parrot tulip companions.

Alliums

I must include alliums here, for they bring simple architectural beauty to the late spring garden for very little outlay. I like to experiment with different sorts, and this year have been entertained by the very gradual development, which started back in February, of *Allium giganteum*, a 120cm (4ft) stem with delicate little pompom heads that seems to attract all the bees in the neighbourhood.

Bees also dangle in profusion from the *Cristophii* alliums, which look like some extraordinary purple star that has fallen out of the sky. I like the way the alliums dry out and yet continue to look arresting throughout the summer. This isn't good if you want more colour next year, but I like to cut the dry flower heads to put in jugs on the table.

Snowdrops

Snowdrops are among the first bulbs of spring to appear. The best place to plant them is under a tree or among the bushes, where they can be left undisturbed. Plant fairly close together about 5cm (2 inches) below the surface.

Narcissus

Narcissus is the correct name for all daffodils and narcissi. Plant from August to November, at a depth three times the height of the bulb. In lawns they are best planted slightly deeper, at a depth of 15cm (6 inches). If your soil is heavy and poorly drained, mix a handful of grit into the base of the planting hole. Try Jack Snipe, a short variety with pointed yellow petals for window boxes and pots.

Crocuses

Crocuses look best when planted in drifts across a lawn. I can't keep my camera lens away from the spectacular displays in the local park, which look like colourful mint humbugs. However, small bowls and flowerpots filled with, say, a white theme look stunning. Plant 5cm (2 inches) deep and fairly close together.

Grape hyacinths

What about the gorgeous cobalt blues of grape hyacinths (*Muscari*)? Try Blue Spike (12.5cm/5 inches), with a delicious fragrance.

One of the greatest treats you can give a friend is a little pot of grape hyacinths (see next page) – cheaper than a bus fare, and if the flowers are still in bud they will bloom for a couple of weeks in a cool room.

SHORTBREAD AND
BUTTERFLY CAKES FOR TEA

Shortbread

This has been a week of a million loose ends and not enough time to tie them up. With such a shortage of minutes I rely even more on the throw-it-together school of cookery. A perfumed aunt is coming to tea and I think she will approve of some easy peasy buttery shortbread. Shortbread is something that should never be bought unless it's one of those proper Scottish varieties with a good proportion of butter in it. Making it is as simple as pressing the mixture into a tin, cooking it, dividing it, leaving it to cool and then eating it.

Variation
For almond shortbread, add 50g/2oz/½ cup ground almonds and use 100g/3½oz/¾ cup flour.

125g/4oz/1 stick unsalted butter, softened
75g/3oz/⅓ cup caster sugar
150g/5oz/generous 1 cup plain flour
extra caster sugar, for sprinkling

Cream the butter and sugar in a bowl with a wooden spoon or mixer until the mixture is white and light and the sugar no longer feels gritty (caster sugar is best, as it mixes quicker than coarser sugars). Mix in the flour, then form the mixture into a smooth ball with your fingertips. Press it into a greased tin and prick it all over with a fork.

Place in a preheated oven, 160°C/325°F/Gas Mark 3, for 25–30 minutes until pale golden. Cut into 8 triangles while warm and sprinkle with sugar. I like to decorate shortbread with lavender or other edible flowers (see page 150). Leave to cool on a wire rack. Keep crisp by storing in an airtight container. I like my shortbread thicker rather than thinner, there's more to get your teeth into. It's always good for a picnic.

Butterfly cakes with orange butter icing
makes 12

On dull Saturday afternoons in 1969, when 'Racing From Doncaster' was the only thing on TV, what else could a 12-year-old do, when she was too young to take the number 49 bus and hang out with the hippies at Kensington Market? Make butterfly cakes, of course. This is a variation on the Victoria sponge idea (see page 151).

110g/4oz/1 stick unsalted butter, softened
110g/4oz/generous ½ cup caster sugar
2 large eggs, beaten
110g/4oz/generous ½ cup self-raising flour, sifted

for the butter icing
75g/3oz/¾ stick unsalted butter
175g/6oz/1½ cups icing sugar
grated rind and juice of 1 orange

Cream the butter and sugar until light and fluffy. Add the beaten eggs, and then fold in the sifted flour with a metal spoon; or, if you have a food processor, process the whole lot. Spoon equal amounts of the mixture into a greased 12-cup bun tin and place in the middle of a preheated oven, 190°C/375°F/Gas Mark 5, for 15–20 minutes, until well risen and golden. Leave to cool.

To make the butter icing: Soften the butter and beat in the sifted icing sugar, adding enough orange juice to give it the right consistency. Add the grated orange rind. It should be thick enough to hold its shape for spreading.

To make the butterfly wings: When the buns have cooled, cut a circle off the top of each, 1cm (½ inch) from the edge. Fill the hole with a dollop of butter icing. Cut the circle in half and position the halves in the cream to look like wings.

FIVE SIMPLE SPRING SUPPERS

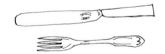

Relieved to put my thick black wool tights at the back of the drawer, and pull on pale denim jeans and a white shirt, I am also conscious that what we eat at the end of the day should be nourishing and filling but have the colour and freshness of the new season.

Toad-in-the-hole

Toad-in-the-hole – sausages baked in a bed of crispy batter – is a hearty (some might say stodgy) supper dish, but a welcome one after a walk in the park with the dog and small children in tow and everyone feeling ruddy-cheeked and famished.

Offset the stodge element with a plate of peas or a crunchy green salad with thinly sliced white cabbage, chicory leaves and watercress, which is now in season. All-year-round demand has rather blurred the boundaries of the natural watercress season, but as the days get longer and the weather gets warmer, the crop will get heavier. For the best mustardy flavour look for the dark green stocky-looking plants; the paler, small-leaved varieties are much milder – more like lettuce.

110g/4oz/generous ¾ cup plain flour
pinch of sea salt
1 egg, beaten
250ml/8fl oz/1 cup water and milk mixed
1 tbsp olive oil
500g/1lb beef, pork or lamb sausages (the best quality you can afford)

Sift the flour and salt into a basin. Make a well in the flour and add the egg and a little of the liquid. Gradually beat in the flour from the sides of the basin and add the rest of the liquid. Beat the batter thoroughly. Heat the olive oil in a small meat tin or dish, then pour in the batter. Slice the sausages in half lengthways and lay them in the batter. Place in a preheated oven, 230°C/450°F/Gas Mark 8, for 35 minutes or until the batter is golden. Turn the tin once while cooking.

This tastes very good with wholegrain mustard and it is important to use good quality sausages with a high meat content.

Simple grilled mackerel

for 6

An oily fish that is full of omega-3 and flavour, mackerel must be bought really fresh, preferably when its skin is still shiny and faintly rainbow coloured.

In the interests of conservation, let alone price, the first wild salmon of the season is almost off limits. (Read how seriously fishing stocks are compromised and find out what fish is ok to eat in Charles Clover's *The End of the Line*[4], and also see the film of the same name). Mackerel, however, is at its best now, and although Clover says *'again far too much illegal fishing and concern about stocks, but a fast-reproducing fish and in a much better state than Europe's white fish'*, it is a fast-reproducing fish and in a much better state than Europe's white fish.

Mackerel needs little embellishment other than salt and a drizzle of olive oil, but its flavour is really brought out if you stuff each gutted fish with some lemon and thyme or parsley, and coat the skin – into which you have inserted a couple of garlic cloves – with Dijon or whatever mustard there is to hand. Grill on both sides for 10 minutes each (or see how to barbecue on page 123). Serve with boiled new potatoes, spring greens, and maybe some spoonfuls of alioli or green sauce (see pages 101).

Smoked mackerel, beetroot and horseradish salad

Also try
Smoked ham is a good alternative to the mackerel if you want a more meaty salad.

The magenta pink of cooked beetroots is visual balm in early spring. I like to arrange them sliced on a plate with a smoked mackerel fillet, chopped spring onions and a large dollop of peppery horseradish sauce. Shop-bought horseradish sauce is ok, but can be very acrid and vinegary. Try this recipe.

125ml/4fl oz/½ cup double cream
50g/2oz/⅓ cup fresh horseradish root, peeled and grated
1 tsp Dijon mustard
2 tsp cider vinegar
sea salt and freshly ground black pepper

Whip the cream and fold in the remaining ingredients.
    Horseradish is also delicious with cold beef. I particularly like it with a plate of roasted veg (see page 206).

Fish and chips

Clues to freshness
This applies to all fish: eyes clear and dark, gills bright red, no odour, the blood should be red and running, the flesh firm; if it is soft, the fish is old and has gone past the stage of rigor mortis.

The other night, with a surprise five extra mouths from work to feed, I swung into action with an all-in-one pan supper: my version of fish and chips, without the labour-intensive and smelly deep-frying.
    Chunks of fish are roasted with potatoes with their skins on, and put on the table in the same pan in which they're cooked – robust, tasty and very much part of my throw-it-all-together way of cooking. Serve with a salad such as tomato, onion and cucumber, chopped finely, or if it's last minute make a mixed salad with whatever is in the refrigerator.

2 tbsp extra virgin olive oil
1kg/2lb potatoes with skins on, sliced into wedges
1 onion, roughly chopped
6 garlic cloves, roughly chopped
800g/about 1½lb salmon fillet (sustainably farmed), haddock fillet or cod
    loins (responsibly fished), skinned and cut into chunks
juice of 1 lemon
handful of parsley, coriander or dill, chopped, to garnish

Put the oil in a roasting pan and add the potatoes, onion and garlic. Place in a preheated oven, 190°C/375°F/Gas Mark 5, for 30 minutes, or until the potatoes are crisp on the outside and tender in the middle, turning the mixture over once or twice. Add the fish chunks and lemon juice and cook for a further 10 minutes.
    Garnish with the parsley, coriander or dill, season and serve from the pan.

Mussels in coriander, ginger, garlic and coconut

serves 4

Mussels are good at this time of year and relatively inexpensive. A big pan of steamed mussels served with salad and hunks of bread and maybe a bowl of rice to mop up the coconut-and ginger-flavoured broth makes a quick supper.

2kg/4lb mussels
1 tbsp extra virgin olive oil
6 garlic cloves, chopped
60g/2¼oz/¼ cup peeled fresh root ginger, grated
grated rind and juice of l lemon
1 glass white wine
400ml/14fl oz can coconut milk
large handful of fresh coriander, chopped
freshly ground black pepper

Scrub the mussels and discard any with broken shells or that do not close when tapped against the edge of the sink (see below). Put the olive oil in a large pan, add the garlic, ginger and lemon rind and juice and cook on a medium heat for about 5 minutes. Add the wine and the mussels. Put the lid on and steam for 10 minutes, or until all the shells are open, shaking regularly so that they're evenly cooked. Turn off the heat. Discard any mussels that remain closed (see below).

Drain the liquid into another saucepan, add the coconut milk and simmer for 10 minutes. Add the chopped coriander. Pour back into the pan containing the mussels, season with freshly ground black pepper and serve immediately. You probably won't need to add salt as the mussel juice will be salty enough.

Preparing mussels

Always buy mussels from a reliable source. Raw mussels should be shiny, mostly unbroken and closed, and generally have a fresh sea smell.

Scrub them well and remove any barnacles and the tough fibrous 'beard'. Throw away any that have broken shells. Open mussels that refuse to close when tapped on the side of the sink are dead: throw them away too. Mussels that remain closed when they have just been cooked were dead before you bought them and should also be chucked out.

Finally, cook mussels for the briefest time – 5 minutes at most, or until they just open. That way, they'll be juicy, sweet and tender.

endive

raspberry

more tomato

Bean green

aubergine

Rose petal

leek green

Violet

pumpkin

Beetroot

Lettuce

watermelon

Cabbage

Good things to eat in summer: tomatoes, rocket, sardines, strawberries, cucumbers, gooseberries, basil, sweetcorn, crab, raspberries, mint, radishes, blackcurrants, figs.

summer

If spring is the season of renewal, autumn of decline and winter of death, then summer is the season of maturity. These are our salad days, when we're at our best. Summer's warmth, light and freedom makes it the most optimistic and celebratory of the seasons. Summer and love have always gone together. In Alexander Pope's poem about summer, the hot season and the hot emotions are all wonderfully entwined. The summer is love and love is the summer. Summer is when we can rewrite the rules of the nine to five routine – maybe lie on a cool sofa, the long afternoon stretching languidly ahead, with little more than an ice-cream and a book to occupy the tastebuds and thoughts. When the sun dips below the horizon, there's summer's night-time agenda: the buzz of nocturnal life (*'sound loves to revel in a summer night'* observed Edgar Allan Poe in his poem *Al Aaraaf*), and with it so many sweet scents and velvet warmth.

SUMMER IS A SALAD OF COLOURS

I can't get enough of the glorious colours that come with summer. The sun lights up and highlights everything, like a natural stage illumination. Sitting at my desk, washed in the bleaching newness of a summer's day, the hot morning rays put an optimistic spin on all the usual desk tasks.

For couscous recipe
see page 94

Summer whites are wonderfully fresh and more invigorating than the softer, mellow whites of winter. It doesn't cost much in time or effort to freshen up a junk table in a coat of white paint and then take it out into the garden as the cornerstone of an informal outside dining space. Once I get started, it doesn't seem much more of a bother to give the same treatment to a pair of junk chairs that have been waiting patiently for some attention. And to make all this whiteness and lightness complete, I want to give the outside walls a summery Andalucian dazzling whiteness. To this end you'll find me mixing up buckets of powdered lime with water, like stirring icing for a cake. Slapped on with a wide, flat brush, this timeless paint effect creates a softer white translucent look as the shadows lengthen.

As I drink something cool under the dappled shade of the apple tree, the summer garden is a glossy, shimmering blaze of pink roses and purple lavender spikes. Looking up at the infinite sky, I want to bring all that fresh summery blueness into the house. I start by spreading the table with blue and white striped fabric or making new cushion covers in cotton faded like blue jeans. Did you know that flies hate blue and that's why kitchens and pantries were once painted in bright blue, and still are in many hot parts of the world? Flies hate basil, too, so little pots of it are placed on the counters of shops and bars in places like southern Italy and Spain.

The palette of food colours in the summer kitchen displays more of the season's visual intensity. Pale soups of garden vegetables take on the hues of summer frocks. Salads look like Impressionist outbursts: lime green stalks and leaves, glowing lemon yellows and beetroot pinks. But the colours that sum up summer on a plate have to be the hyper reds, pinks and oranges of tomatoes. At any other time of year such shocking shiny colours would have the sensitively attuned reaching for their dark glasses.

A SLICE OF SUMMER

Natives of South America, tomatoes were not grown in England until the late 16th century. Known as *pommes d'amour* – love apples – tomatoes acquired a reputation as an aphrodisiac in some parts of the country.

My nose recalls the green herby smell of the knobbly tomatoes we grew in Spain, hanging like fat shiny jewels from leafy waist-high plants on twiggy supports, with skins that turned from salmon pink to carmine streaked with yellow under the hot sun. The seeds would arrive in a jam jar, handed over by one of the old flat-capped boys in the village.

The variety? Nameless, it had been grown for ever, each year's crop contributing to the new seed of the next. The sweet flesh was a constant at each summer's local harvest, when bubbling oil drums of water set over a fire would sterilize jars for the chopped tomatoess. Those plump beauties are my blueprint for the perfect tomato. They're hard, I'd venture impossible, to find among the pumped-up, bland and watery hothouse types sold all year round. But at least in summer the hothouse-grown are a little sweeter and softer, yielding to the touch.

My experiments with growing seeds saved from Spain have been dismal. Maybe this failure to thrive is based on the same principal as local wines not travelling well. Because sunshine and heat are unreliable elements of the English summer, I tend to stick to smaller plum and cherry varieties, little yellow ones even, which ripen more quickly. (There might be wonderful recipes for green tomato jam, but I prefer tomatoes fresh, pink and juicy.)

Good ideas for summer tomatoes

At their simplest, all fresh sweet tomatoes need is a little sea salt to bring out their flavour, with maybe a few torn basil leaves (tearing retains their pungency). Oregano or marjoram leaves are a delicious companion too. When adding tomatoes to salads, rather than cutting them into wedges, tear them into pieces for a more natural look, especially if all you have are the rather uniform ones from the chiller cabinet. Keep tomatoes at room temperature and their flavour will improve. Over-ripened ones can still be roasted in the oven with garlic and olive oil, 40 minutes at 190°C/375°F/Gas Mark 5, or made into pasta sauce (see page 82).

Gazpacho

Only the English drive along a bleached motorway when the sun is high in an old Mercedes without air conditioning, but what do you do when there are building supplies to buy or in-laws to collect? In our years of Spanish travels, there were many car events like this with hot, sweaty, irritable children, and adults, to pacify.

The pit stop at a roadside bar or service station is the lifesaver, and even the least appetizing menu (over-salted and anonymous meat stews come to mind) is bound to be redeemed by the inclusion of a cooling bowl of gazpacho. Its taste, texture and colour is never uniform, but reflects the cook's particular style – probably the way his/her family has been making it for generations. Whether it's thick, chunky and tomatoey red, or a smooth orange-pink, flecked with green herb colours, this classic Spanish cold summer soup is made up of such simple, everyday fresh ingredients that it's hard to wreck.

Similarly, when it comes to doing it yourself in the kitchen, you won't go wrong as long as you use ripe tomatoes and good olive oil.

1kg/2lb ripe tomatoes
1 cucumber, skin on, roughly chopped
4 garlic cloves, roughly chopped
100g/3½oz/scant 2 cups fresh breadcrumbs
4 tbsp extra virgin olive oil
2 tbsp sherry vinegar
salt and freshly ground black pepper

To remove the skins, pierce the tomatoes and put them in a pan of boiling water for a minute or so. Take them out, cool them under a tap and peel off the skins. Roughly chop the flesh. Put all the ingredients except the salt and pepper in a bowl and liquidize – I use an electric hand whizzer – until smooth. Season to taste.

Chill in the refrigerator and, if it's a very hot day, serve with ice cubes. Small bowls of chopped pepper, onion and cucumber are a crunchy and tasty garnish.

If the gazpacho is too thick, add a little water.

Bread and tomato
pan con tomate

Toast rubbed with oil and garlic and heaped with fresh tomato is an Andalucian bar staple that we also like to make for breakfast, lunch or just as a snack on a summer weekend. It's similar to the Catalan *Pa amb tomàquet,* where a sweet ripe tomato is squashed onto toasted bread until its juices soak the dough. Other southern European tomato experiences include Provençal *Pan bagnat,* a kind of Salade Niçoise in a bap, and Italian panzanella (see page 95), a moist tomato and bread salad.

To make *pan con tomate*: Simply toast slices of a good quality sourdough or rustic bread (have a go too with bread from the recipe on page 198) and then rub with garlic and extra virgin olive oil. Top with fresh tomato (scoop out and use the insides only). Season with freshly ground sea salt and black pepper.

I keep olive oil in a little metal jug with a thin spout, a basic kitchen item from many Spanish hardware shops.

Tomato sauce

This rich, garlicky tomato sauce has endless uses, including serving with pasta, as an accompaniment to a bowl of couscous, or the base for pizza (see pages 201–204). You can also freeze it.

3 tbsp extra virgin olive oil
10 garlic cloves, roughly chopped
1kg/2lb ripe tomatoes, skinned (see page 79)
salt and freshly ground black pepper

In a saucepan, heat the oil, add the garlic and cook for 5 minutes or so, until soft, then add the tomatoes and season to taste. Cook on a low heat for about 45 minutes, until the mixture is reduced and is a smooth-ish mass of tomato.

In winter I substitute fresh tomatoes with tinned, which have a better flavour than tasteless out of season tomatoes. A couple of tablespoons of tomato paste will intensify the tomato flavour.

Fried tomatoes

These are great at breakfast time with all the usual fry-up elements such as eggs, sausages and bacon.

Cut your tomatoes in half and fry, flesh side up, in half extra virgin olive oil and half unsalted butter. Cook on a low heat for 10–15 minutes on each side. Season with salt and freshly ground black pepper.

THE HERB GARDEN

Hardy perennial herbs that will keep coming up each year:

mint, chives, thyme and lemon balm.

I have been pretty gung-ho with my herb planting and I hope for the best, but if I were starting all over again I'd read Jekka McVicar, the last word on herby matters. She suggests that a herb garden should have an area in full sun and another in semi-shade. If you can't have both in one spot, go for two small dedicated areas. Partial shade is good for salad and annual herbs because it protects them from the midday sun and helps prevent the soil from drying out; full sun is best for Mediterranean herbs such as thyme because it helps bring the essential oils to the surface of the leaves, intensifying the taste.

A salad bowl of herbs

Chives

The bulbs multiply easily, so divide clumps each year for more supplies in the garden. The onion-flavoured leaves and flowers can be eaten whole or as a garnish to flavour salads, crème fraiche and soups. Bees love the flowers too.

Rosemary

Rosemary is a perennial herb, which loves sun and hates boggy or wet soil, as I have discovered in the part of the 'potager' that is the lowest lying and where all the water collects in winter. Only a few metres away, in a drier section, I have to restrict the vigorous spurts of growth that the rosemary makes there every summer.

The delicate blue flowers are as pretty as they are a magnet for every bee that finds itself in our garden. I cut sprigs to flavour everything from roast chicken to potatoes and fish. It is also a wonderful herb to weave into an aromatic wreath for Christmas (see page 253).

Rocket
(see right)

Rocket's bitter, peppery flavour transports me to an Italian holiday I enjoyed as a 17-year-old, on an 'exchange' learning to ride pillion in a bikini. I was given the task of picking the straggly dandelion-like leaves from a scrubby patch outside the back door for salad that was tossed in golden olive oil after courses of pasta and grilled meat. It's really easy to grow, and another rampant self-seeder, so don't let the plants flower unless you want them to. One packet of seeds, sown directly into the ground in spring, produces a prodigious supply for our summer salads.

Basil

An annual herb, the mint/anise/clove taste of basil is intense. Ilse Crawford's book *Sensual Home*, records that designer Ettore Sottsass describes '*basil flavoured architecture*' as a way of expressing so much with so little. From scattering a few young basil leaves on a tomato salad, to torn basil leaves in stylist Nathalie Hambro's sandwich of wholemeal bread, cream cheese, tomatoes and walnut halves, it is one of summer's essentials.

Sow the seeds in spring and throughout the summer. It is temperamental, hates to be watered at night, and won't tolerate cold or extreme heat. It will wilt during the day in full sun.

Try sweet Genovese basil, perfect in pots, grown on a sunny windowsill. It's a traditional fly repellent too, and for this purpose pots of basil are still common on shop counters in Spanish villages.

Coriander

Coriander is an annual, which can be sown in spring. Trim regularly if you want the leaves, leave alone if you want the seeds. The parsley-like leaves with a sharp citrus flavour go so well with roasted vegetables (see page 206) and in Mussels in coriander, ginger, garlic and coconut (see page 72).

Thyme

An evergreen perennial, thyme has the kind of delicate flowers and leaves that you see on 18th century sprigged fabrics and wallpaper. I use sprigs of lemon thyme to decorate lamb chops or grilled fish.

Dill

Dill is easy to grow from seed. The feathery anise leaves are delicious with fish, especially salmon (gravlax), and the seeds can be used in vinegars and teas. Dill likes the sun.

Bay

Bay can be trimmed into simple topiary shapes. The leaves give a really rich taste to meat stews and fish. Use sparingly as it has a very strong flavour.

Sage

A perennial with silvery grey-green leaves. Sage tastes good with fried eggs (see page 46), pasta and risotto and is used in stuffing (sage and onion) for poultry. Like thyme, it dries well.

Oregano

A perennial you can sow by seed or divide by root cuttings. Oregano's pungent flavour is delicious with tomatoes, fish and meat and, like rosemary, it can survive in a poor soil.

Marjoram

Marjoram is from the same family as oregano, and will grow as a perennial in full sun. It's good in stuffings for meat, rubbed into meats before roasting, or added to tomato sauce. Even after last winter's frozen ravages, I notice that these two herbs have regenerated without fuss.

Spearmint

As soon as the first sprigs of spearmint (garden mint) appear, they're snipped and tossed in the pan with new potatoes, or used in just about every summer salad that appears at my table. It has such an aromatic and refreshing flavour. There's the pleasure too, of cooling mint tea after supper, or as a reviving drink first thing (see page 43). It's a vigorous self-seeder so I pick it freely.

I also grow basil mint, which is a curious combination of mint and basil flavours, and is quite a good substitute for fresh basil when you're making a tomato salad, say. However, given half a chance it will take over the garden, so keep cutting it back. Mint likes sun and a rich wet soil.

Lemon balm

Another wild child of the herb garden, but I make a feature of mine and trim them into leafy balls, topiary style. The broad lemon-scented mint-like leaves are delicious as a tea, chopped in a salad, stuffed whole in fish, or used to decorate a lovely summery pudding of meringues and cream.

French tarragon

A hardy perennial that can be propagated by cuttings. Its strong aniseed flavour is delicious with a cream sauce that's combined with pieces of either roasted or pan-fried chicken (see page 206).

Herb garden punch

Adapted from *The Times Cookbook$_6$* by Frances Bissell.

2 sprigs each of French tarragon, mint and basil
600ml/1 pint/2½ cups water
250g/8oz/generous 1 cup caster sugar
50ml/2fl oz/¼ cup white rum
25ml/1fl oz/⅛ cup Cointreau
juice of l lime and l lemon
fizzy water, to taste

Put the herbs and water in a saucepan and boil for 3 minutes. Strain the liquid into a jug and stir in the sugar. Leave to cool, then refrigerate until needed. To serve, mix with all the remaining ingredients.

Herbs in pots

Herbs that will thrive well in containers: oregano, sage, thyme, chives, basil, curly parsley, rosemary, chervil, dill and rocket.

Simply growing a row of herbs on a windowsill or the summer's supply of basil in a flowerpot connects you to the earth. For wooden boxes, drill holes in the base for drainage. Punch a few drainage holes into some heavy-duty plastic and line the box before adding soil. For a zinc bucket, drill a few holes in the base and cover loosely with broken flowerpot shards to aid drainage.

When replanting a pot of herbs, use a pot one size bigger. Half fill the new pot with potting compost, put the plant in the pot and fill the space around the root ball with the potting compost. Water well.

SALAD DAYS

I love the laziness of summer salads, tossing fresh leaves with a simple dressing, chopping the bright stems and sweet roots of the season, using up leftovers, almost without intention creating brilliant palettes of edible colour for the table.

A Pure Style version of Salade Niçoise

serves 4

The great food writer Elizabeth David once said that there are as many versions of Salade Niçoise as there are cooks in Provence, but in whatever way it is interpreted it should be a simple, country salad. It usually contains lettuce hearts, black olives, hard-boiled eggs, anchovies and sometimes tuna, with garlic in the dressing. My version depends upon what's in the vegetable basket – new potatoes, French beans, tomatoes, even slivers of carrot. Not everyone in the family gets on with salted anchovies and capers or caperberries are a piquant substitute.

The recipe below is a robust holiday lunch idea, which can be made to stretch further with bread, butter and a hunk of Manchego cheese.

The addition of barbecued or grilled fresh tuna (try to buy a more sustainable variety*) makes it especially delicious. If fresh isn't available, it's perfectly ok to substitute with tinned tuna – the all-important thing is to have a garlicky dressing or alioli to go with it.

*Sustainable tuna:
Try to buy Albacore (pole and line, handline or troll-caught from the South Pacific or South Atlantic) or skipjack (pole and line or handline-caught from the western and central Pacific or the Maldives).

500g/1lb/2¾ cups cooked green beans, cut into manageable pieces for a fork
400g/13oz tuna steak, barbecued (see page 122) and cut into small cubes
4 hard-boiled eggs, peeled and cut into quarters
80g/3oz/¾ cup caperberries
sea salt and freshly ground black pepper

Place the beans in a pile on each plate and top with the tuna, eggs and caperberries. Season to taste. Pour on the dressing just before eating or serve with a separate bowl of alioli (see page 101 for recipe).

Roast beetroot, lentil and goats' cheese salad

serves 4

500g/1lb/2½ cups beetroot
200g/7oz/2½ cups cooked green lentils
2 red onions, finely chopped
3 tbsp balsamic vinegar
4 tbsp extra virgin olive oil
100g/3½oz soft goats' cheese, crumbled
handful of mint leaves
sea salt and freshly ground black pepper

Also try
Chopped roasted beetroot with chopped raw tomatoes, carrots and red onions make a wonderful pink/red/orange combination, and is incredibly healthy too.

To roast the beetroot: Put it in a roasting pan, cover with foil and place in an oven preheated to 190°C/375°F/Gas Mark 5, for about 45 minutes. Top and tail the knobbly ends, then peel the beetroot and cut it into chunks. (The almost indelible lipstick fuchsia pink juice from beetroot is a fantastic way to add colour where you don't want it, so do all the peeling and chopping by the sink – or in it, to be safe!)

Combine all the above ingredients, season to taste, and serve as a lunch or supper idea on its own, or as a salad to go with grilled fish or meat.

Mozzarella and rocket salad

Mozzarella
Originally called *mozza*, this soft, fresh Italian cheese was traditionally made with buffalo milk, but is now made almost exclusively from cows' milk.

I know it might be a bit lah-di-dah to say that packet mozzarella won't do, but so many of the packet varieties are tasteless and almost as plastic in texture as their wrappers. If you can, it really is worthwhile spending more for a freshly made buffalo milk mozzarella in its own bath of milky liquid to keep it moist. Creamy and mild flavoured, it will almost melt in your mouth, and is the perfect foil for a scattering of slightly bitter and aromatic rocket leaves (see page 86).

Dress with a few drops of extra virgin olive oil and some salt and pepper – a squeeze of lemon juice is delicious too.

Couscous with roasted veg and fresh mint

serves 4–6

(see page 76)

Couscous is a kind of hard wheat semolina, which has been ground and then moistened and rolled in flour. It's the most popular food in, and the national dish of, Morocco, Algeria and Tunisia, and is also traditionalal in Sicily. The grain is steamed and served with a stew or broth or with a garnish and there are sweet couscous dishes.

The name is said to come from the French pronunciation of the word '*suksoo*', which describes the sound the vapour makes when it passes through the grain as it steams. Almost all the couscous available here, though, is commercially pre-cooked and only needs water adding.

Do try and catch the vibrant film *Couscous, La Graine et le Mulet*, about a family of North African émigrés in France. Drool over the visuals of preparations for *couscous aux sept légumes*: gorgeous steaming piles of fluffy grains, spicy sauces, vegetables, glistening fish and wonderful cooking pots, all washed down with plenty of on-screen family tension and squabbling.

A quick but delicious way to eat couscous is to combine the cooked grain with a mixture of roast and raw vegetables and herbs. This is a sublime salad to eat with meat or fish, or on its own.

Added zing
Another delicious addition to the couscous is a handful of chopped preserved lemons.

3 red or green or mixed peppers, chopped
3 onions, chopped
2 aubergines, chopped
handful of garlic cloves, roughly chopped
6 tbsp extra virgin olive oil
300g/10oz/2 cups couscous
rind and juice of 1 lemon
2 tbsp chopped parsley
2 tbsp chopped mint
2 tbsp chopped coriander
salt and freshly ground black pepper

Place all the vegetables and the garlic in a roasting tray. Mix with 2 tablespoons of the olive oil, season and place in an oven preheated to 190°C/375°F/Gas Mark 5, for 45 minutes. Place the dried couscous in a bowl, cover with enough boiling water to submerge the grains, and leave for a few minutes before fluffing up with a fork.

Add the roast vegetables to the couscous together with the rest of the olive oil, the lemon rind and juice, and the parsley, mint and coriander. Season to taste.

Panzanella

serves 4–6

(see next page)

Just as we make an everything-in-the-refrigerator kind of salad in order to use up leftovers, so the wonderful Italian panzanella dish with leftover bread is another familiar idea on the summer table.

Traditionally it includes sliced bread and fresh tomatoes, flavoured with basil, olive oil and vinegar. Ideally, the bread used should be saltless Tuscan bread made in a wood oven and between a day and a week old.

But this is a moveable feast, as long as you use ripe sweet tomatoes and decent rustic-style bread – maybe an old ciabatta loaf or some sourdough. I don't like mine too soggy and so hold back on the tomato if it looks as if it's heading that way.

200g/7oz stale bread such as ciabatta
1kg/2lb ripe tomatoes, torn, not chopped
½ cucumber, roughly chopped
1 onion, roughly chopped
handful of parsley, roughly chopped
handful of basil, roughly chopped
2 garlic cloves, roughly chopped
6 tbsp extra virgin olive oil
2 tbsp balsamic vinegar
sea salt and freshly ground black pepper

Tear the bread into chunks and put in a bowl with the tomatoes. Mix and leave for 15 minutes to let the bread absorb the tomato juices.

Add all the other ingredients and serve.

EASY DRESSINGS

*'Let the salad maker be a spendthrift for oil, a miser for vinegar,
a statesman for salt and a madman for mixing.'*
Spanish proverb

Vinaigrette dressing

Traditionally one part vinegar to three parts oil, you don't actually have to use vinegar at all in an oil and vinegar dressing. A squeeze of lemon juice is often enough to give it the right piquancy if your oil is a very good extra virgin variety (see page 100) and you don't want it drowned. On the other hand, rich balsamic vinegar can be very sweet and taste good all on its own with a little salt and pepper on a salad of green leaves, or trickled over roasted vegetables.

A simple Pure Style dressing

In a small bowl, with a fork, mix 1 tablespoon of sherry vinegar, with 1 tablespoon of wholegrain or Dijon mustard and 2 finely chopped garlic cloves. Add 2 tablespoons of extra virgin olive oil, whisking all the time until you have an emulsion. Add salt and freshly ground black pepper to taste.

Variations on olive oil: use walnut oil for a nutty flavour. Rapeseed oil is smooth and more delicately flavoured than olive oil.

Variations on vinegar: balsamic vinegar is rich in flavour and texture. Pomegranate molasses from my local Turkish deli is another sweet and rich vinegar substitute.

Mixed chopped herbs: basil, tarragon, chives.

Simon's tomato, lime and red onion salsa

A crunchy, piquant salad with a vibrant colour, perfect for spooning on a plate with fish. Combine finely chopped tomato, red onion and parsley with lime juice and some seasoning.

Emma's green sauce

serves about 6

Emma passed on this tangy idea to me, which can be thrown together very quickly using a hand whizzer.

Hard-boil a couple of eggs, chop them roughly and add to a bowl with 100ml/ 3½fl oz/6 tbsp plus 1 tsp of extra virgin olive oil, the juice of 2 lemons, chopped leaves from a bunch of parsley and a handful each of capers and small gherkins.

Mix well and season to taste with sea salt and freshly ground black pepper. Pour half the mixture in a bowl and whiz until smooth. Combine the two and serve in a bowl or jug for everyone to help themselves.

Hollandaise

Also try
Add chopped tarragon for sauce béarnaise or chopped garlic for a garlicky version.

This hot butter sauce is the perfect match for some young sprouting broccoli spears, served as a starter or with roast meat or fish. You'll need a bowl (stainless steel, ideally, but not vital), a saucepan into which it will fit, and a wire whisk.

1 tbsp water
2 egg yolks
100g/3½oz/scant ½ cup unsalted butter, cubed
lemon juice, to taste
sea salt and freshly ground black pepper

Half-fill the saucepan (see introduction) with water and bring to the boil. Turn the heat down so that the water simmers, and place a heatproof bowl (see introduction) on top. Pour in the water and egg yolks and whisk until creamy.

Add the butter cubes, one at a time, letting each one melt before you add another. Keep whisking until thick and creamy. Season with sea salt, pepper and lemon juice to your liking.

If the sauce is too thick, add a little more water.

In order to lessen the risk of the sauce curdling: keep the water below the boil, and make sure it doesn't touch the base of the bowl.

If it all goes wrong and starts to curdle, remove from the heat and start the process again with a beaten egg yolk in the bowl. Slowly add the curdled mixture and put it back on the heat, whisking madly; you should be able to rescue it. You won't be able to do anything with it if it gets too hot and coagulates into scrambled egg.

Mayonnaise

Once it is made, keep mayonnaise away from extremes of heat, cold and agitation.

Mayonnaise requires some physical vigour with a wire whisk or wooden spoon. The oil is all important as far as flavour is concerned. You should use a sweet, clean-tasting olive oil, such as Brindisa's Arbequina. Many virgin and extra virgin oils are too strong, hot and throat-grasping for the purpose. You can also blend a bland oil such as sunflower with an extra virgin oil for a smoother taste. Oil connoisseurs will no doubt be horrified by the suggestion but it will make for a gentler taste.

1 large egg yolk, at room temperature
150ml/¼ pint/⅔ cup extra virgin olive oil
1 tsp lemon juice
sea salt and freshly ground black pepper

Put the egg yolk in a bowl and beat for a minute. Put the oil into a jug (I use a Spanish metal olive oil tin with a long thin spout) and pour it, drop by drop, whisking all the time. Once it thickens (after you've added half of the oil), you can pour in the remaining oil in a thin trickle, whisking all the time. When nearly all the oil is used, add a little lemon juice and whisk until the mayonnaise is stiff (and like Elizabeth David's *'beautiful shining golden ointment'* in *French Provincial Cooking₇)*. If the oil is added too quickly the mayonnaise may separate, but save it by starting again with a yolk in a new bowl and slowly beating in the separated sauce.

If using a food processor, blend the yolk and add the oil in a thin trickle while the blade is turning. Season with sea salt and freshly ground black pepper to taste.

Green mayonnaise

Steam a handful of young spinach leaves, some tarragon leaves and a few sprigs of parsley for a couple of minutes. Drain, whizz with a hand blender and mix the purée into mayonnaise. It looks very beautiful – pale, green and speckled. Serve with fish, grilled meat and raw vegetables.

Alioli
(see opposite)

I make this garlicky and glossy mayonnaise throughout the summer to eat with everything from plain boiled potatoes and raw vegetables to grilled fish and meat.

4 garlic cloves (less if you don't want it so garlicky)
1 large egg yolks, at room temperature
150ml/¼ pint/⅔ cup extra virgin olive oil
1 tsp lemon juice
sea salt and freshly ground black pepper

Make this like the mayonnaise above, but pulverize the garlic cloves and stir them into the egg yolks before you start to add the oil.

I pound the garlic cloves with a wooden pestle and mortar, another of my cheap and cheerful kitchen utensils, before adding them to the bowl or basin for the rest of the process. Don't overdo the lemon juice as the alioli should be nice and thick.

THE SIMPLE SUMMER PICNIC

Hard-boiled eggs and cold sausages on wet Sunday afternoons in my parents' Cortina, or crowding in the shade on sandy towels after a swim and tearing off sweet mouthfuls of bread, cucumber and papery thin ham: this is the stuff of summer picnicking. I like the idea, too, of freedom, that you can eat very delicious things of your choice, when you want to – rather than suffer inedible overpriced rubbish on the plane, for example.

I always take a bread bun or two with a plump tomato and a few basil leaves to get me through to touchdown. (Knives and airport security are not compatible, but the edge of a debit card has proved to be a useful cutting tool.)

Heat, dust and tortilla

Useful picnic kit
twists of paper with salt and pepper
bottle opener with knife and fork combined
beach umbrella in thick fabric to stop you burning underneath
plastic bottle of frozen water

Use a metal storm kettle for places with a fire risk: *fill the kettle with water, light a small fire in the base with a sheet of newspaper followed by small twigs, cones, dry grass or even animal dung.*

Civilized picnics require minimum fuss. A cotton cloth for spreading on the ground and sandwiches wrapped in a sheet of crisp greaseproof paper are simple luxuries. Some of the more essential picnic features include a cold bottle of fizz in an insulating bag for adults, and non-melty, non-sticky, non-gooey things such as seedless grapes, sticks of carrot or hunks of plain cake, for children.

For colour, sweat, dust and the opportunity to drink quantities of *fino* sherry and lemonade *rebujitos* without falling off your mount, the village pilgrimage on horseback to the *hermita* at Alájar in Andalucia is a real picnickers' picnic.

We awoke with the birds at 5am and struggled into flounced flamenco dresses hung up the previous day to preserve their creases. Plaiting hair, fixing flowers and strapping little heeled flamenco shoes onto a sleepy five-year-old isn't easy when tripping over the enormous frilly skirt of your own hip-hugging blue-and-white spotty number.

We saddled up in the stable yard, hazy and dark, with shawls and jumpers to keep off the early morning chill. Violet, a quiet, shabby donkey, carried two straw

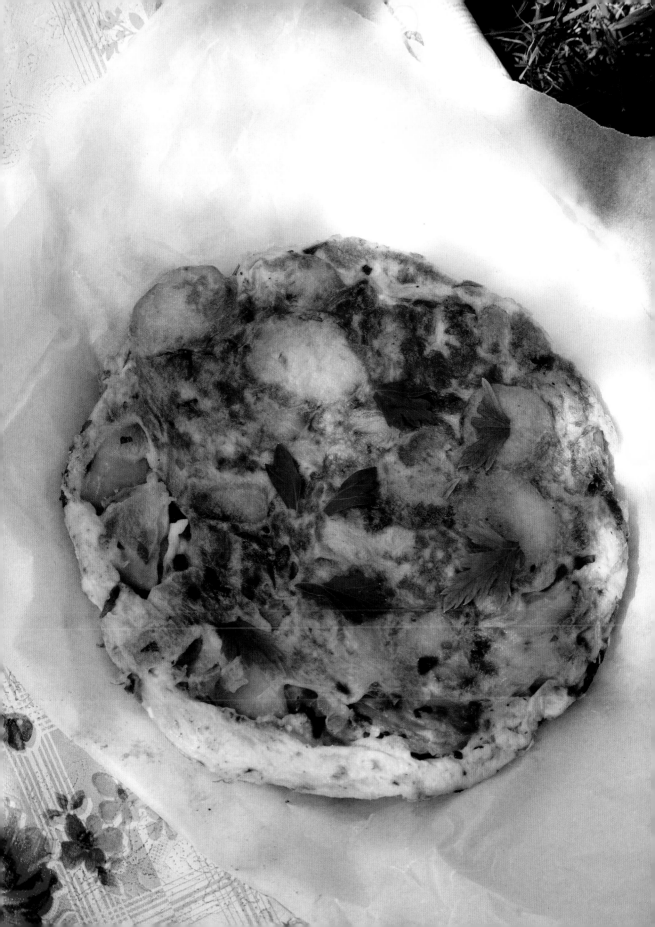

panniers on her back with our picnic contributions: tortilla, slices of *jamón* and three plastic bottles of gazpacho frozen overnight so that by the time we needed them they would still be cool enough to drink, despite the searing lunchtime heat, (even in early September).

Up in the saddle, clip clop clip clop, all in rhythm to meet the glow of daybreak and the air, fresh with lavender and herby cistus. We soon joined the main procession – a straggly ribbon of horses, carts, people on foot, and at the head two oxen straining with the Virgin – which, hours later, after many stops for drinking and dancing, swept into the *hermita*, where everyone made camp under the olives, in dappled shade, as if in a painting by Goya.

The back-to-nature element of the event was underlined later that night, when I was stepping out of my limp and dust-drenched finery – a shiny black scorpion scuttled from the discarded folds, and met its end with a child's riding boot.

Tortilla de patatas
Potato omelette
serves 8

(see previous page)

The fabulous thing about tortilla is that there's no end to the possibilities of shape and size. Chunky slices as thick as cake or thinner and more delicate offerings are equally acceptable. We continue to make tortilla, for picnics in London parks or a day out at the sea. The secret is to keep it wrapped in greaseproof paper or tinfoil. Don't squash it and if it's really warm day the tortilla should be put in a cool box.

This recipe can be prepared the day before and stored in the refrigerator.

4 tbsp extra virgin olive oil
2 large onions, sliced
4 garlic cloves, roughly chopped
6 potatoes, peeled and diced
10 large eggs, beaten
handful of parsley, roughly chopped
sea salt and freshly ground black pepper

Heat the olive oil in a medium-sized nonstick frying pan. Add the onion and garlic and fry gently for a few minutes until softened. Add the potatoes, cover and cook on a moderate heat for about 25 minutes until soft, stirring from time to time to prevent the onion from browning.

Add the beaten egg and chopped parsley and season to taste. Lower the heat and use a spatula to define the edges of the tortilla.

Just before the top layer is cooked, remove from the heat and turn over: place a plate on top of the pan, flip over, then slide the tortilla from the plate back into the pan. Cook for a few minutes until golden brown. Serve hot or cold.

Beach picnic

Packing up a beach picnic of rolls is a daily routine on holiday. The only rule is that lettuce and tomato components are taken along in a separate bag or a box and added at the last minute on the beach, as the rolls get very soggy if they are overloaded with the more watery of salad stuffs.

Crisp on the outside and chewy inside, bread rolls from the *panaderia* are slit open and spread with egg mayonnaise, which involves little more than mashing up hard-boiled eggs with a spoonful of mayonnaise or the alioli (see page 101) left over from supper, parsley or coriander, salt and pepper. Another idea is to substitute the mayonnaise with crème fraîche.

Tuna mayonnaise

Substitute the hard-boiled eggs with drained canned tuna, and mix with the same cast of ingredients as above. We also add lemon juice and sometimes a couple of mashed anchovies.

Hummus

Another favourite is to wrap up oatcakes or pitta in foil, for dipping in a pot of hummus. I like my hummus roughly textured, but if you prefer it smoother simply whizz it for longer. Also good with hunks of cucumber, carrots or raw peppers.

400g/14oz can chickpeas, drained and rinsed
200g/7oz/scant 1 cup tahini
3 or 4 garlic cloves
4 tbsp extra virgin olive oil
juice of 2 lemons

Whizz all the ingredients together with a hand blender.

THE HOLIDAY COOK

Go armed with a local cookbook, for ideas
In Spain one of my favourite sources is Maria Jose Sevilla's *Spain on a Plate,* and in Portugal *The Algarve Fish Book* by Nico Böer and Andrea Sierbert barely leaves the work surface, so informative is it on fish and how to cook it.

I know that staying in hotels provides tremendous rest and respite from the daily round of domesticity, and I wouldn't exactly say no to a night or two with crisp linen and room service. But cooking for yourself with fresh local ingredients, in a rented house or apartment, is another way of winding down because you get closer to the essence of the place you've travelled to.

You get to see how a place ticks, buying fresh bread alongside wiry fishermen or bundling plump tomatoes, squeezed and personally approved, into the trolley bag, just like a local housewife. I have one of those wheeled accessories that Olhãon locals trundle over cobbles to the daily fish and vegetable market. Saturday is best, when local farmers bring their own produce and I come back with exquisite olives, sprigs of mint, strings of garlic and brilliant zinnias, one euro a bunch. In the fish market there's a fresh ozone sea smell and wet tiled slabs displaying everything from anonymous *pescada*, one euro per kg, so ordinary it doesn't deserve a name, to sardines, so fresh and firm they look as if they're swimming in shoals across the counters.

Oscar's fish soup

serves 4

When you're on holiday with keen cooks, there's a chance to learn some new tricks in the kitchen. My friend Oscar's deliciously simple fish soup endears him to anyone he stays with. It is based around tomatoes, wine, saffron, oregano and chilli and whatever fish is fresh and available.

After a gentle amble around Olhão fish market and several thick black coffees, Oscar arrives with clams and a kilo of mixed fish pieces for *caldeirada*, Portuguese fish stew (see page 108 for a recipe). He disappears into the kitchen to sort the clams, and remove bones and skin from chunks of monkfish, ray, dogfish and hake. Half an hour or so later, apron fetchingly tied, Oscar emerges triumphant with a pot piled high with glistening fish and plump clams in shells steamed open, all drenched in a glorious pink soup that has a satisfying herb and chilli kick. Back home in London I try Oscar's soup, adding a few tablespoons of fish stock (see page 236) to some prawns, haddock and salmon from the local fish shop, and am surprised that even if it doesn't have the high quality fishy ingredients I can get in Portugal – it has evocative fishy flavours of the sea and summer.

2 tbsp extra virgin olive oil
1 onion, roughly chopped
4 garlic cloves, roughly chopped
2 piri piri peppers, finely chopped (or a few dried chilli flakes)
1 x 175ml wine glass white wine
1 tbsp dried oregano
3 or 4 filaments of saffron (toasted beforehand, see page 134)
1 bay leaf
400g/13oz ripe tomatoes, skinned, cored and chopped
1kg/2lb mixed fish pieces (whatever is available on the day)
500g/1lb/2 cups clams
large handful of coriander, chopped
sea salt and freshly ground black pepper

Heat the oil in a large, deep pan and gently fry the onion, garlic and piri piri peppers for a few minutes, or until soft. Add the wine, oregano, saffron, bay leaf and tomatoes and simmer for 10 minutes.

Add the fish, and a little water if it is too thick, and simmer for another 10 minutes (depending on the type of fish), until cooked through. Add the clams (prepared as on page 114), put the lid on and steam for another 5 minutes, until open. Discard any that do not open. Stir in the coriander, season and serve.

This soup can be served with toasted bread smeared with garlic and tomatoes (see page 82), and garlicky alioli (see page 101) for stirring in.

Caldeirada de peixe
Portuguese fish and potato soup

I make this robust and delicious fisherman's soup with *caldeirada* (mixed fish) on the stove, in a heavy-based, flameproof terracotta casserole dish from the local Olhão hardware shop. You can use any deep pan or pot with a heavy base. Back in England, I substitute the Portuguese fish with cod, haddock, salmon or whatever happens to be available.

Start by frying some garlic and onions and a couple of piri piri peppers in some olive oil. Add thinly sliced potatoes, roughly chopped red pepper and ripe tomatoes (use canned ones in winter), and a layer of fish.

Repeat this alternate layering until the dish is full. Top with salt and freshly ground black pepper, a bay leaf, 3 or 4 strands of saffron, a handful of coriander and parsley and a generous slug of white wine. You need plenty of liquid – add some water if you need to. Cook until the potatoes are tender.

Traditionalists will not stir the pot, but I think that a gentle prodding isn't out of order to make sure that the contents don't stick and burn on the bottom. All in all, this takes about an hour to cook on a medium heat, depending on the size of the pan. Serve with a green salad or a plate of steamed green beans.

SUMMER FUEL FOR BEACH GAMES

In the spirit of Minnie Aumonier, who declared that *'when the world wearies and society fails to satisfy, there is always the garden'*, I look for pasta sauce ideas when I lose inspiration in the kitchen during the never-ending school holidays. A table of the hungry hordes demands plenty of pasta carbs and generous helpings of grated Parmesan.

Whatever pasta is on the boil (spaghetti and linguine are the favourites), the larger the pot the better, so you can swirl it all about and stop it sticking. A little oil in the water will also stop it boiling over and making a mess on the stove.

Georgia's pesto

During one recent hot and steamy holiday on Long Island in America, while eating beads of golden corn, punnets of dewy blueberries and cooling Sugar Baby watermelons, my daughter Georgia mastered the art of making pesto with the lush basil from our hostess's veg patch. We ate it stirred into heaped bowls of spaghetti on the porch watching the fireflies dancing at dusk.

100g/3½oz/1 cup pine nuts
handful of basil, finely chopped
1 garlic clove, chopped
half a handful of grated Parmesan cheese
150ml (5fl oz) extra virgin olive oil
sea salt and freshly ground black pepper

With a hand whizzer, grind the pine nuts until no whole ones are left, and then add the basil, garlic and Parmesan. Mix together, adding olive oil until the pesto is able to slide off a metal spoon. Season. Stir into hot, freshly drained spaghetti, and top with more Parmesan if needed.

**Puttanesca
sauce**

serves 4

A rich, hot and tasty sauce, with the flavours of black olives, salty anchovies, tomatoes and capers.

6 tbsp extra virgin olive oil
8 canned anchovy fillets, chopped
2 garlic cloves, roughly chopped
1 dried red chilli or piri piri pepper, crumbled
400g/13oz tomatoes
100g/3½oz/⅔ cup black olives, stoned and sliced
1 tbsp capers
400g/13oz spaghetti, freshly cooked and drained
handful of parsley, roughly chopped
sea salt and freshly ground black pepper

Heat the oil in a large frying pan and cook the anchovies, garlic and chilli/piri piri pepper for a couple of minutes. Meanwhile, drop the tomatoes in a bowl of boiling water and leave for 1 minute. Rinse them under cool water, then skin them, core them and chop the flesh. (Use canned plum tomatoes if good fresh ones are not available.) Add the tomato flesh, olives and capers and cook for a couple of minutes more. Season as necessary. Stir into the pan the spaghetti and parsley. Cook for 1 minute, stirring to mix thoroughly. Serve immediately.

Book food

Sometimes there's nothing better after a hellish day than a solitary bowl of pasta, in bed with a book. Alan Bennett's hilarious memoirs and Sarah Waters' creepy Gothic thriller *The Little Stranger* are recent companions.

I drain some pasta, put it back in the pan, stir in crumbled goats' cheese, a couple of fresh chopped tomatoes, extra virgin olive oil, chopped parsley and finely chopped garlic, and cook for a couple of minutes or so.

CLAMS IN BUCKETS
AND FORAGING BY THE SEA

The day the Luftwaffe shot up the beach, my 10-year-old dad was on the rocks throwing skimming stones at blue basking sharks. With nature posing less of a threat than the wartime activities of humans, it was quite usual for my grandmother to let him roam the tideline. The rock pools were teeming with shrimps then, and my dad would take them home to boil for tea. There were buckets of seaweed to lug back, too, to spread as fertilizer at the bottom of the bean trenches.

Years later, dad, as hunter-gatherer, would poke around the shorelines on family holidays to Brittany and Bordeaux. Squatting together on a rock one blazing afternoon, me in one of my mum's home-sewn frilly bikinis, he handed over a dripping and fleshy oyster. I was too mistrusting of its fishy strangeness to accept his offer of another one but, along with tasting my first fat penny bun, a wild mushroom, or making salads from dandelion leaves, it got my interest going in foraging for wild things.

Foraging for shellfish

See also Preparing mussels on page 72.

Down by the sea, there are shellfish (mussels, oysters, clams and razor shells), leafy greens and seaweeds to be discovered.

I'll start with health and safety, which for once is not namby-pamby. You do not want to eat a bad oyster or mussel, for example. Both can be easily contaminated, even when living in what is technically good and clean 'category A' sea water.

Speak to the locals and check out the regulations – there are minimum sizes and a limit to the number of live sea animals you can gather. Find out where you can safely forage, as some areas may be out of bounds and you will need permits.

Steamed clams

serves 4 as a starter

Our clam-foraging holidays in Portugal begin on the chuggy ferry to the beach, passing fields of sand delineated by small rocks and marker posts, where storks creep and seagulls swoop around an enduring expanse of blue sky. Figures bent double are using rakes to expose clams, which they plop into little buckets and sell to local restaurants.

The children have spent many summers trawling through the sand with their hands, protective shirts billowing in the shallows, for their own catch of clams. Put in one of those large plastic flagons and covered with seawater, they are fresh for when we eat them for supper at home in the indigo twilight. Here is a very simple way to cook them.

1kg/2lb/4 cups clams
3 tbsp extra virgin olive oil
6 garlic cloves, roughly chopped
2 tbsp white wine
squeeze of lemon juice
handful of coriander, chopped
freshly ground black pepper

First discard any broken or open clams, and clean the rest.

Use a big enough saucepan so that the clams are comfortably spread, rather than heaped up – this will help them to open more easily.

Heat the olive oil and cook the garlic for a few minutes. Add the white wine and a squeeze of lemon. You won't need salt or more water as there is salty liquid in the shells. Season with pepper.

Add the clams and chopped coriander, put on the lid and steam for 5 minutes or so, until all the shells are open. Chuck away any unopened ones.

Pour onto a large dish to let everyone help themselves – and have extra bowls to hand for the empty shells, and bread to mop up the juices.

Razor shells

You would be very unobservant not to see the empty razor shells scattered on the sand like old-fashioned cut-throat razors. They are underrated by the English, but a favourite of the Spanish and Portuguese, who scoff them in huge quantities. I first ate them in a bar in Madrid, and despite a slightly off-putting chewy quality, they have a lovely delicate fishy flavour.

Razors live in sand, so when you see an indentation and a hole in the sand, pour a little salt into the hole and wait – after a few minutes the razor will come up to the surface and can be pulled out.

Razor shells with lemon and parsley
serves 2

This is based on a recipe I discovered in the National Trust's *Wild Food*[8]:

12 razor shells
½ dsp unsalted butter
zest and juice of ½ lemon
handful of parsley, roughly chopped
freshly ground black pepper

Clean the razor shells (see the method for cleaning mussels on page 72) and discard any that are broken or that do not close when tapped against the side of the sink. Put them in a pan with the butter and lemon zest and juice. Add the parsley, cover the pan and simmer for a couple of minutes; any longer and they tend to get tough. Season with pepper.

Put on a plate and pour over the juices. Discard any that fail to open. Serve with hunks of bread.

Sea urchins

Perched gingerly on the edge of a little blow-up dinghy with three Italian friends, I discovered that the sea urchin's fierce black quills don't protect it from being eaten by greedy beachcombers.

We prised them off the rocks with a knife, quite a feat if you don't wear gloves, sometimes going overboard with a snorkel to get really choice ones a few feet down. Soon there was a great pile of the spiky creatures around our feet. Maria Fausta's dad expertly sliced them in half and we scooped out the sublimely flavoured orange-coloured roe – a teaspoon at most – to eat with little bits of bread and shots of white wine in humble plastic cups.

According to Nico Böer and Andrea Siebert, authors of *The Algarve Fish Book*, Dalí and Lorca were said to have been fed on this phosphorous-rich food, which is only found in appreciable amounts during a full moon. If you don't believe this, open one the day after: you'll find the shell completely empty.

Sea beet

This is found on upper beach paths and cliff tops. It's thought to be the ancestor of most, if not all, cultivated varieties of beet, from beetroot to sugar beet. The leaf tastes like spinach, but doesn't collapse into a pulp quite so quickly on cooking. The best time to pick sea beet is in April and May, when the sweeter new growth appears, but in sheltered areas it's possible to collect enough for a meal at any time of the year.

Sauté the leaves in butter until just wilted and still bright green. Add lemon juice, salt and pepper, and serve with grilled fish.

Bladder wrack

This is common and grows on rocks between the low and high tide levels. Gather the fresh plants that are still attached to the rocks, dry them in the sun and break them into small pieces to add to fish soups and stews.

Sea lettuce

If you can get over the fact that this is the same green slimy weed that rather unpleasantly flaps around your feet in the shallows, it is tasty. I came upon this simple recipe in Roger Phillips' *Wild Food*:

25g/1oz sea lettuce
Japanese rice vinegar
1 tbsp sukiyaki sauce

Wash and place the sea lettuce in a small bowl and cover with rice vinegar. Put the sukiyaki sauce in a separate bowl. Take pieces of sea lettuce and dip in sukiyaki sauce. Good served with some rice, too.

Sea greens

Marsh samphire is found in salt marshes and mud flats. Neither cactus nor seaweed, this fleshy genus is a member of the goosefoot family.

When you come across a large crop, it looks like a green meadow. Picking it is a muddy affair – a knife or scissors are recommended to leave the roots intact and it rarely reaches collectable size until late June, with midsummer day being the traditional start of the season in Britain.

Eat the young tips, which lack the central tough fibre, either raw in salads or lightly steamed and served with fish.

COOKING ON THE FIRE

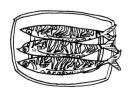

Barbecuing is a manly, caveman activity, which for a very long time I was shy about attempting. When you're around a man who is barbecuing, he can become tetchy and mutter and swear when the meat catches fire or he drops a steak by accident into the dog's waiting jaws. I have therefore associated barbecues with stress, bad language and charred food.

However, being marooned with large groups of starving teenagers on holiday, I have become quite adept with the charcoal – but not without spying on the techniques used by the doorstep barbecuers of Olhão.

To light a barbecue

Wear an old pinny or apron; barbecuing is a greasy, sooty job if you're new to it. You don't need a fancy, all-singing all-dancing, Dallas-style contraption. I use a very basic metal Olhão model, crib shaped, on four legs, with an adjustable rack and a wraparound windshield – it cost about 17 euros.

Put card or newspaper underneath the barbecue – if the floor is terracotta and absorbent, oil splatters are not very sightly. Have a cup of water handy to douse the flames that flare up when fat drips on the charcoal. A sliced potato put on the grill will also help damp them. The best tools are a long barbecue fork and tongs.

Arrange the charcoal in a pyramid shape, Girl Guide campfire style. Insert three firelighters (biodegradable ones coated with vegetable oil are less noxious) evenly spread into the pyramid, and light with a match. Leave for 20–30 minutes, by which time the flames should have died down and the charcoal will be grey. Spread the charcoal more evenly and you can start to cook.

Other key points are that thin pieces of meat, fish or vegetables need a higher heat for a short period; thick pieces – including spatchcocked chicken or bigger fish such as mackerel – need the opposite.

Don't attempt to barbecue in the dark – it's impossible to see whether anything's cooked properly or not. Rig up lanterns, or if you're out in a field get someone to point a torch.

Cleaning a barbecue
For cleaning the barbecue I recommend hot water, detergent, a stiff wire brush and thick gloves, and try to do it regularly. It is a very unpleasant chore if you're dealing with layers and layers of burnt-on fat.

Grilled squid
(see previous page)

Once you get past the sliminess of the preparation, squid is the most delicious treat, with a sweet, light fishy flavour. I buy medium-sized squid, allowing one per person.

First, take out the transparent quill. Pull off the outside membrane and cut off the two wings. A firm tug on the head will separate it from the body, along with the rest of the innards, leaving the body an empty white sack. (If the ink sack bursts don't be alarmed; rinse off the ink under a running tap.)

Remove the beak and cut away the tentacles. Cut the body in half lengthways, and open it out flat. Score the body in a criss-cross pattern with a sharp knife, to keep the flesh tender when it's being cooked. Marinate the body, wings and tentacles overnight in the refrigerator in olive oil, lemon juice and chopped garlic, parsley and coriander.

Put all the marinated pieces on the grill and cook for 2–3 minutes on each side, until they are lightly brown and crispy on the outside. Serve with wedges of lemon and alioli (see page 101).

Sardines

The daily catch in Olhão is so gleaming and rigid with freshness that there's no need to gut them. I use a wire fish holder, which means I can turn them over all at once. I grill them for a few minutes on each side, until the eyes turn white and opaque and the skins are lightly browned.

Salads to eat with sardines include my take on Italian panzanella (see page 95), made with stale bread, chopped tomatoes, cucumber, onion, parsley and a dressing made with oil, balsamic vinegar and garlic. Then there are lemon quarters to squeeze over the fish and bring out its flavour.

Tuna

A grilled tuna steak can be horribly dry if you don't marinate it for a couple of hours in oil, lemon juice, garlic, sea salt and freshly ground black pepper, and if you don't cook it in nice thick slices. By thick, I mean about 4cm (1½ inches). I like the fish to be brown and toasted on the outside, 4–6 minutes each side, with a pink middle.

Serve with alioli (see page 101), a green salad and good bread, or cut it into chunks to incorporate into a salade Niçoise (see page 89).

Mackerel
(see Simple grilled
mackerel page 71)

Gut the fish (insert a sharp knife into the ventral part, cutting from front to rear,
and carefully pull out the internal organs, trying not to pierce the liver or
gallbladder) or get the fishmonger to do it for you. Rinse the inside thoroughly.
Stuff it with slices of lemon and sprigs of herbs such as tarragon, dill or coriander.
Make slits in the flesh and insert thin slivers of garlic. Sprinkle with sea salt.

To make cooking easier and stop the skin from sticking to the grill, insert the
fish into individual wire fish holders, and cook for about 10 minutes on each side
on a medium heat until the fish is cooked all through to the bone and the eyes are
opaque and white.

Piri piri chicken
serves 4

Necklaces of dried red piri piri peppers are sold in the market in Olhão, for making
hot piri piri sauce to coat chicken and make it taste spicy and even more delicious
on the grill.

for the chicken
**whole chicken (about 1kg/2lb), spatchcocked (this involves removing the
backbone and sternum of the bird and flattening it out before cooking –
if you're not sure, ask the butcher to do it for you)**

Oven roasting
If you run out of heat
on the barbecue, move
the chicken to a
roasting pan and cook
at 190°C/375°F/Gas
mark 5 in the oven for
about 30 minutes, until
the juices run clear
when the thickest part
is pierced with a skewer.

for the piri piri marinade
**4 piri piri peppers, roasted (10 minutes at 190°C/375°F/Gas Mark 5),
peeled, deseeded and finely chopped**
juice of 1 lemon
4 garlic cloves, chopped
1 tbsp parsley, chopped
1 tbsp paprika
4 tbsp extra virgin olive oil
sea salt and freshly ground black pepper

For the piri piri marinade: Combine all the ingredients and pound to a paste in a
pestle and mortar or with a hand whizzer. Brush the chicken with half the
marinade, cover and leave in the refrigerator for a couple of hours.

Put the meat on the barbecue and cook for about 15 minutes on each side,
basting regularly with the rest of the piri piri marinade. I find tongs in one hand
and a long fork in the other are the best tools for handling chicken. Ensure the
chicken is cooked through. The juices should run clear when the bird is pierced in
the thickest part of the thigh with a skewer; any sign of pink and it needs cooking
for longer. I cut the chicken into pieces with scissors and serve on a big plate for
everyone to help themselves.

Beefburgers

makes about 8 burgers

Serve with mustard, Green mayonnaise (see page 103) or tomato ketchup for those who can't do without their fix. Wedge with crunchy green salad between bread buns or pitta bread. Serve alongside a more substantial salad such as Couscous with roasted veg and fresh mint (see page 94).

Beefburgers can be rustled up at the last minute.

1 large red onion, chopped
2 spring onions, chopped
handful each of parsley, coriander and basil, roughly chopped
1kg/2lb/4½ cups good minced beef
2 eggs
sea salt and freshly ground black pepper

Add the red onion, spring onions and herbs to the minced beef with the eggs and mix the whole lot together. Add the seasoning. Mould into 8 round burger shapes with your hands.

Cook on the barbecue for about 4 minutes, then turn and cook for 4 minutes on the other side. This is for burgers that are rare inside, how I like them. Double the cooking time if you prefer them well done.

Grilled vegetables

We barbecue everything from slices of courgette or aubergine to tomato halves. The important thing for flavour, and to help stop the vegetables from sticking, is to marinate everything in a little oil, lemon juice, garlic, sea salt and freshly ground black pepper beforehand (up to an hour or so in the refrigerator).

If you can get them, those delicious long thin green peppers, which are plentiful in southern Spain and Portugal in the summer, need only a few minutes cooked whole; their skins should be lightly charred on the outside.

Bananas in pyjamas

Adults might like to add rum (or Cointreau or brandy) with the butter and sugar.

I haven't got into cooking sweet stuff on the barbecue – partly because I think the essence of barbecuing is all about the delicious meaty or fishy charred smell of savoury things. I will make an exception, though, for 'Bananas in pyjamas', an old family favourite that is good when you've finished all the main cooking but the charcoal is still hot enough for a last blast.

Place the bananas in their skins on to the grill. Cook them until brown on the outside and soft inside. Slit all the way down one side and fill with butter and brown sugar (and rum if you're an adult), and scoop out the melty gooey sweet insides with a spoon.

COOL FOOD

Keep cool under a billowing blue and white striped canvas awning
It isn't difficult to construct. Hem the raw edges and punch metal eyelets in the four corners of the fabric. Secure the awning to hooks on the wall with rope or fabric ties threaded through the eyelets. If there is a summer thunderstorm, it can be taken down quite quickly.

During our ten summers of Spanish siestas, when the dogs were flopped under the water tank and the bees buzzed around the eucalyptus flowers, the only way to keep cool inside was to batten down the shutters. If for some reason we didn't, the house would be hot and oppressive, the refrigerator straining to keep its innards cool.

But if the shutters could be flung wide open when the worst of the heat had diminished, cooler, jasmine-scented air wafted in to refresh us all – supplemented by something cool and fruity to drink and eat for pudding.

Salads of colour

Fruit, fruit and cream, cream and fruit: these are my favourite ingredients for cool summer puddings.

When there are so many delicious fruits in season, it isn't necessary to spend hours on fancy puddings. A simple combination in pinks and summer whites – watermelon, honeydew melon, pear and mint leaves in a marinade of orange and lemon juice – looks and tastes so of the moment.

Or how about a bowl filled with slices of yolk-yellow peaches and plump carmine cherries coated in grated ginger, orange juice and dessert wine? Sometimes, we just do a fruit salad version of whatever is left over in the refrigerator and throw in handfuls of toasted pinenuts or almond flakes for added texture.

The main things to remember are that the fruit should be in easily spoonable pieces and, if the weather is very hot, chill the fruit salad beforehand in the refrigerator – it will taste fresher and crisper. I serve fruit salad with anything from crème fraîche and cream to ice-cream, sorbet or shortbread, to make it a little bit more filling.

Meringues, raspberries and cream

makes 12 meringues

Leftover egg yolks
Use up the egg yolks
in lemon curd (see
page 246 for recipe).

Pile up a plate of meringues wedged with whipped cream and raspberries and you have a simple and elegant pudding.

Successful meringues depend upon a little bit of lemon juice added to the egg whites to help them get really stiff in the beating; a well-oiled or greaseproof-papered tray to stop them sticking; and a long, languid stay in a low oven, two hours or so, so that they are crunchy outside but still a little bit chewy inside.

3 egg whites, at room temperature, separated
175g/6oz/generous ¾ cup caster sugar
½ tsp lemon juice
300ml/½ pint/1¼ cups double cream, whipped
200g/7oz/1½ cups raspberries

Make sure the mixing bowl is very clean and the eggs are at room temperature. Whisk the egg whites until stiff. I use an electric whisk for ease. Add a quarter of the sugar and all the lemon juice and keep whisking until the mixture holds its shape – this will take a good 5–10 minutes.

Gently fold in the rest of the sugar with a metal spoon. Put dollops of meringue onto a baking sheet lined with lightly oiled greaseproof paper – you want 12 meringues in all – and leave in the middle of an oven preheated to 140°C/275°F /Gas Mark 1, until set, as described above.

To construct the pudding: Combine the cream and raspberries in a bowl and wedge pairs of meringues together with a large dollop of the mixture. Pile these pyramid-style on a plate or cake stand.

Raspberry fool

serves 4

Serve from the refrigerator in simple glasses with chunks of shortbread (see page 68) and sweet wine.

225g/7½oz/2 cups raspberries
90g/3¼oz/scant ½ cup caster sugar
300ml/½ pint/1¼ cups double cream

Hull and wash the raspberries. Mash the berries with a fork and stir in the sugar. Whip the cream until it forms soft peaks. Add the mashed raspberries a spoonful at a time to the whipped cream. Refrigerate until needed.

Gooseberry fool

Simmer 225g/7½oz/2 cups of topped and tailed gooseberries in 90g/3¼oz/scant ½ cup caster sugar for 3–4 minutes or so, until soft. Whizz to a purée with a hand blender, leave to cool, then stir into 225ml/7½fl oz/1 cup whipped double cream, as above.

Lemon ice cream

Lemon ice-cream is dead easy, and you can give it a nice twist by sandwiching spoonfuls between those delicious toffee wafers imported from Holland.

3 lemons
200g/7oz/1 cup caster sugar
450ml/¾ pint/2 cups double cream

Finely grate the rind of 1 lemon. Squeeze the juice of all 3 lemons and combine with the sugar. Whip the cream and fold into the sugar mixture. Pour into a shallow container and freeze until solid around the outside and mushy in the middle. Stir with a fork and freeze again until firm.

Homemade lemonade

Summer is the season for wearing loose shifts, and dressing furniture in cool white cotton loose covers (see previous page), perfect textures on which to siesta until late afternoon. There are cooling drinks of iced water from the bottle kept in the freezer or a glass of homemade lemonade.

5–6 lemons
4 tbsp sugar
1 litre/1¾ pints/4 cups cold water
1 lemon, thinly sliced
sprig of mint

Squeeze the juice from the lemons.
    Dissolve the sugar in the pan with 100ml/3½fl oz/½ cup water. Cool, then add to the lemon juice with the remaining water. Add the lemon slices and leave to marinade overnight in the refrigerator. Serve with lots of ice and a sprig of mint.

SOMETHING TO BRING BACK HOME

The days of hauling a case of wine into the overhead cabin locker are dim and distant. Even taking home a pot of orange blossom honey in the hand luggage is a no-no.

Score brownie points with foodie friends by bringing home a box or two of pure Portuguese sea salt, which as yet is not counted as a potentially dangerous substance. It might seem a touch rarefied to debate the qualities of one of the most basic items in the store cupboard, but the fast-flowing commercially produced stuff that you pick up at the corner shop tastes rather unpleasant compared to a pure, mineral-rich sea salt.

There's something much more mellow and flavour-enhancing about pure sea salt. And it couldn't be a more sustainable commodity, produced by little more than water, sunshine and wind.

I use flakes of *flor de sal* to flavour salads, and to sprinkle finely on the top of grilled fish. The coarser *sal grosso* crystals are perfect for dissolving in soups, stews, water to cook pasta in, and so on.

Saffron

A box or jar of saffron filaments is another favourite edible and lightweight treasure to take home. The earthy, bittersweet flavour of saffron is as beguiling as its strong smell and gorgeous yellow colour. Saffron is the name given to the three dried red-coloured stigmas, and part of the white style to which they are attached, of the autumn-blooming, purple-flowered crocus. The dried stigmas are known as filaments or threads; they must be rehydrated or powdered before use to release the properties they contain.

A few toasted filaments added to anything from mashed potato to fish stock can enhance every flavour. I use it to colour and flavour grains such as rice and couscous. In Morocco saffron is added to a tagine of lamb. I have been inspired to crumble a few filaments into a slow casserole, or pieces of chicken roasting in a pan.

Saffron worldwide:

Spanish *azafrán*
Catalan *afra*
French *safran*
Italian *zafferano*
Portuguese *agafrao*
Swedish *saffran*
Finnish *sahrami*
German *Safran*
Dutch *saffraan*
Turkish *zafaren*
Vietnamese *cây nghé tây*

Be careful when buying saffron filaments abroad, as much of it will be safflower, and the huge pile of yellow powder sold as *azafrán* in a local Mediterranean market will be turmeric. I buy Spanish saffron from good food shops when I am in Andalucia, although not at the airports where it is very expensive.

Prepare the saffron either by grinding the filaments into a powder after toasting in a pan or by infusing them in some hot water. In John Humphries' *The Essential Saffron Companion,* there is a delicious-sounding recipe for saffron tea.

Salty tales

On one of those afternoons when a fierce south-westerly whips sand around the ankles and makes beach activities harder work than simply honing one's tan, I would suggest a visit to Rui Simeão's salt ponds in Tavira in Portugal. There they are, glistening pools with beds of baked clay, on the watery horizon.

The saltern has been in the Rui Simeão family for over a century, but the Algarve's hot dry summers and tidal waters have made the perfect conditions for salt production – a process of concentrating and evaporating seawater – since as far back as the time of the Phoenicians.

Rui's *marotes* – salt harvesters – bring in the salt between June and September, when there is enough heat and sunshine for evaporation and concentration of the white salt crystals that form on the bed of the ponds.

Sal grosso are coarse salt crystals, delicious for flavouring everything from water for cooking to soups. But for a really fine melt-in-your-mouth quality and texture, there is *flor de sal*. These are the flaky salt crystals that form on top of the thick brine as the seawater evaporates and are scooped out daily using finely meshed sieves.

Because *flor de sal* floats on the surface like cream on milk, it is also known by the salt gatherers as *nata do sal*. It's much more expensive, but is really worth buying for not only looking rather lovely – crystalline and delicate – on, say, a tomato salad, but also for enhancing the tomato's flavour without being overpoweringly salty.

And you probably wouldn't think so, but salt production is as prone to the fickleness of the weather as any other type of farming – one recent season's salt crop was destroyed in a violent summer storm. Even more of an excuse for stocking up the cupboard!

TEALIGHTS, TAPAS AND SUMMER GARDEN SCENTS

The holiday mood continues on dusky summer evenings in London. It's good to make the most of balmy weather and scented roses, lavender and nicotiana. These heady delights are more than enough of a reason to put on an impromptu party.

The kitchen table is heaved out and joined to the wooden garden table to make one long surface. White cotton cloths are spread over them both. We arrange the mishmash of chairs so that they look attractive in their mismatching and set the table simply – tealights in glass jars, glasses filled with roses.

We fix screws in the fence and the back wall to provide support for a long length of wire upon which we hang a row of lanterns. Fairy-like and atmospheric at night, this is an effective, simple and cheap outdoor lighting idea. Metal garden buckets are requisitioned as bottle coolers and we fill them with water and ice, bought in bulk from the off-licence to chill the booze more quickly. Plan B if it rains is to move the show inside and to carry on partying.

The menu features easy-to-assemble salads (see page 91), and maybe a baked fish or piece of meat. Or we prepare some plates of tapas on a tray, to serve with glasses of crisp *fino* sherry or cold rosé.

Easy meat and fish for outdoor eating

A 1.5kg/3lb salmon or trout, scaled and gutted and wrapped in foil with butter or olive oil and stuffed with herbs such as dill, parsley or coriander and hunks of lemon, will take 50 minutes in an oven preheated to 150°C/300°F/Gas Mark 2.

If you want something more meaty, season and sear a 1.75kg/3½lb boned and rolled sirloin of beef in a large frying pan preheated with 1 tablespoon of olive oil. Brush the beef with 3 tablespoons of wholegrain mustard, and then transfer it in the frying pan if it has a heatproof handle or in a roasting tray if it doesn't, to an oven preheated to 190°C/375°F/Gas Mark 5, for about 40 minutes for beef that is rare and red inside, 50 minutes for medium done or 55-60 minutes for well done. Let it rest in the pan or tray for 15 minutes before carving into thin slices. Serve with more mustard and salad.

Tapas ideas

Summer is so suited to idling with almonds, olives and *patatas* alioli, or a little plate of Padrón peppers.

Tapas can be as minimal or as extensive as the mood takes you. It's a great way of turning a quick drink into more of an occasion, and also a stylish and simple way of feeding larger groups of people without turning the event into a catering drama.

Padrón peppers

Smart London tapas bars are serving these small green peppers, which are mild – except for every now and then, when you find one that's really hot.

Grow them yourself, buy them online, or if you are in Spain or Portugal they're a fairly regular fixture in the shops and vegetable markets.

3 tbsp extra virgin olive oil
200g/7oz/1 cup Padrón peppers
sea salt or *flor de sal*

Heat the oil in a pan and fry the peppers for a few minutes until the skins blister and turn brown. Season with sea salt or flakes of *flor de sal* (see page 134) and eat while piping hot.

Quails' eggs

Find these pretty speckled miniature eggs in good farm shops and supermarkets. Boil for 3 minutes and serve with *flor de sal* and freshly ground black pepper.

Garbanzos con espinacas
Spinach and chickpeas

250g/8oz/2 cups fresh spinach, washed
4 tbsp extra virgin olive oil
5 garlic cloves
4 tsp ground cumin
500g/1lb canned chickpeas, drained and rinsed
sea salt and freshly ground black pepper

Steam the spinach for a few minutes in a covered pan with 150ml/¼ pint/⅔ cup boiling water. Drain and set aside.

Heat the olive oil in a frying pan and gently fry the garlic and cumin for a few minutes. Add the chickpeas and cook gently for a few more minutes. Stir in the spinach and cook gently for 10 minutes. Season to taste and serve hot.

Aliño de pimiento
Marinated roasted peppers

This can be prepared the day before and stored in the refrigerator.

4 red and yellow peppers
4 tbsp extra virgin olive oil
4 garlic cloves, roughly chopped
sea salt and freshly ground black pepper

Remove the stalks and seeds from the peppers and slice into 4 pieces. Sprinkle with 2 tablespoons of the olive oil and scatter over the garlic. Roast in an oven preheated to 150°C/300°F/Gas Mark 2, until soft, turning often.

Cool and slice into slivers. Pour over the remaining oil and season to taste.

Patatas alioli
Potatoes with garlic

500g/1lb potatoes
5 garlic cloves, chopped
4 tbsp olive oil
2 tbsp lemon juice
handful of chives, chopped
salt and freshly ground black pepper

Boil the potatoes in salted water for about 20 minutes, until cooked through. In a bowl, crush the garlic to a paste and add the olive oil, slowly beating until it thickens. Add the lemon juice and chives. Mix in the potatoes and season to taste.

Marinated olives

250g/8oz/2 cups olives (try Spanish manzanilla, arbequina and pelotin olives)

for the marinade
1 tsp thyme, finely chopped
1 tsp rosemary, finely chopped
1 tsp ground cumin
2 bay leaves
6 cloves garlic, peeled and roughly chopped
6 tbsp sherry vinegar

Place the olives in a bowl. Mix together the marinade ingredients and pour over the olives.

Mix well and cover with foil or clingfilm. Leave to marinate, covered, in a cool place or in the refrigerator for at least 2 days.

Salted almonds

serves 4

200g/7oz/1 cup raw almonds
some flakes of *flor de sal*
a little extra virgin olive oil

Place the almonds on a baking tray. Sprinkle with *flor de sal* and a little olive oil. Grill until browned and toasted, turning occasionally. Be vigilant because they burn easily.

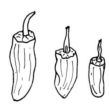

A SUMMER ROSE

Rosehip syrup

2 litres/3½ pints/8 cups
   water
500g/1lb/2½ cups
   rosehips
500g/1lb/2½ cups sugar

Bring 1.5 litres/2½ pints/
6 cups of water to the
boil, add the rosehips
and return to the boil,
cooking until soft.
When cool, strain
through a muslin jelly
bag into a bowl. Return
the pulp to the pan and
add the remaining
water. Bring to the boil,
then cool. Strain
through the jelly bag
again. Pour the extracted
liquid into a clean pan,
add the sugar and boil
rapidly until syrupy.
Pour into sterilized
bottles and keep in
the refrigerator.

Roses are as intoxicating visually as they are sensually, and for very little outlay any gardener can suffuse an outdoor space, no matter how compact, with gorgeous scented blooms in summer. Flowering diminishes, but often stretches way beyond the season.

Right up until last December, for example, with the garden preserved in ice like frozen aspic, I snipped a frosted powder puff of pinky petals from the Eglantine standard. A welcome task repeated well into January.

Any rose lover can enjoy the massed blooms of wild roses in the hedgerows and on motorway banks. Look out for the single delicate white or pink sweet flowers of *Rosa canina*, the most common of the 14 wild English rose varieties.

Also perfumed are the white-flowered field rose, smelling of honey, and the sweet briar, with its fragrant deep pink flower and leaves that, when rubbed, smell of apples.

Not only a source of colour and scent, wild roses kept the population going during the war, when 500 tons of rose hips were collected from the hedgerows during 1943, yielding the equivalent in vitamin C content to 25 million oranges.

In full bloom

My experience of growing roses is that, as long as they are well fed and ruthlessly pruned in winter, they will give fabulous displays year after year. All of the roses I planted six years ago, when we moved house, are doing really well, and unbelievably there have been no casualties, apart from some black spot. They're mainly old-fashioned scented varieties, and pink, just because I find the colour compelling with the lavenders and greens of the garden backdrop, and love the blasts of pink in jugs and vases around the house.

Greenfly
A diluted spray of washing-up liquid deals with greenfly on roses.

First to bloom in my garden are the shocking pink rosette flowers of Gertrude Jekyll, whose scent is strong and fragrant. Although this is a shrub rose, it can grow as a climber. Fanning out the stems on supporting wire encourages even more flowers. Constance Spry (see page 146) is also an old rose hybrid with blousy, clear pink blooms and a strong spicy fragrance, which is heightened after a summer downpour. It climbs along my fence, where there are also the deep pink blooms of John Clare, a lightly fragrant shrub rose.

There are four rose standards at the centre of the potager, creating a miniature orchard of romantic blooms: Eglantine is sweetly scented with soft pink flowers; Mary Rose flowers all summer, with rosy pink flowers that smell of honey and lemon; Winchester Cathedral has white flowers with an old rose fragrance; and a Crocus rose gives a spreading mass of creamy blooms.

There are white climbers, too – Madame Alfred Carrière on the north-facing back wall, and Iceberg, with big white bursts of bloom, outside the kitchen window, both of which I was inspired to plant after visiting the iconic white garden at Sissinghurst, Kent, designed by Vita Sackville-West.

Rose notes

The oldest of garden roses

Gorgeous Rosa Mundi, crimson striped with white, with a delicious fragrance.

Climbers for shade

Madame Alfred Carrière, New Dawn.

Shrub roses for shaded positions

Gertrude Jekyll, Crocus rose.

Roses for pots and containers

It's best to choose shorter varieties, although it is possible to use English climbers such as Gertrude Jekyll if you have a very large container.

Roses for hedges These may be mixed in with normal hedge plants or used as a flowering boundary: Mary Rose, Winchester Cathedral, *Rosa rugosa*.

Climbers and ramblers For growing through trees and covering ugly surfaces: Kiftsgate, Rambling Rector.

Roses for arches You need to use reasonably restrained growing varieties, or else the arch will be overwhelmed. Climbing roses, such as Teasing Georgia, are best because they repeat.

For fragrance Gertrude Jekyll, Strawberry Hill, Constance Spry, Eglantine.

For rosehip syrups and jellies Rambler Francis E Lester, shrub *Rosa rugosa* and *Rosa rugosa* 'Alba'.

Flower power

While a few flowers have real flavour (most notably nasturtiums and pot marigolds), their main attraction lies in their colour. Small flowers and those with no hard parts can be used whole, but with any daisy-like flowers the petals should be pulled off gently and sprinkled over whatever they are being used to decorate.

Gather flowers early in the day when the dew has just dried on them. Cut carefully and keep them on a flat surface. If necessary wash them gently, lightly patting them dry with kitchen paper. Keep them in a closed bag in the refrigerator until needed. Refresh before using by dipping them in ice-cold water.

Edible flowers

Hollyhock	Use the petals in salads.
Daisy, wild and cultivated	Little white lawn daisies made into chains to decorate a cake or flowers tossed into a salad.
Borage, brilliant blue flowers	Sprinkle in fruit salad or in homemade lemonade (see page 133).
Pot marigold	Ancient medicinal and culinary use in baking, in salads for seasoning.
Lavender	Should be used sparingly as strong tasting, although salads were traditionally served on beds of lettuce and lavender sprigs.
Geranium, both flowers and leaves	Can be used in salads. The leaves of the sweet-scented oakleaf geranium can be used to flavour jellies and sponge cake. A circle of six or eight leaves is arranged on the bottom of the tin and the mixture poured in. After baking the leaves may be removed or not. See opposite for a sponge cake recipe.
Primrose	Bright yellow decoration for Easter cakes and biscuits.
Nasturtium	Vivid orange, red or yellow flowers; the seeds are pickled like capers and the leaves have a peppery taste.
Violet	Small and exquisitely formed, violet flowers used to be eaten raw with lettuce and onions; use to decorate homemade biscuits and fairy cakes in spring.
Rose	Petals of all roses, wild and cultivated, which can be used as a simple idea for decorating a summer birthday cake.

A summer birthday cake

(see previous page)

The ratio of ingredients – equal parts sugar, eggs, self-raising flour, butter – is the formula for baking a sponge cake. Baking is all about ratios, and all pros and seasoned home cooks know their proportions.

If you're a beginner this is one of the most useful recipes to keep in mind. You never know when being able to bake a cake will come in handy: a teenager armed with the skill will score highly with parents if he or she can make something for tea at a friend's house.

250g/8oz/2 sticks unsalted butter
250g/8oz/1¼ cups caster sugar
5 large eggs, beaten
250g/8oz/1¾ cups self-raising flour

Cream the butter and sugar together until pale and fluffy; beat in the eggs; fold in the flour with a metal spoon. Pour the mixture into 2 well-greased 18cm (7-inch) tin and place in the middle of a preheated oven, 180°C/350°F/Gas Mark 4, for about 40 minutes. Test with a skewer – if it comes out clean, it is done.

Turn out the sponges on to a wire rack and leave to cool. Sandwich together with a layer of jam and whipped cream inside, and decorate with a layer of cream on top. Use rose petals for decoration (see page 147).

For a lemon icing

150g/5oz/1¼ sticks unsalted butter
300g/10oz/3 cups icing sugar
grated rind and juice of 1 lemon

Melt the butter with the icing sugar and lemon rind and juice. Mix until smooth either in a processor or by hand with a fork.

Sandwich the sponges together with a layer of icing and use the remaining icing to cover the cake, using a palette knife.

151

Potpourri

Bring the scent of flowers, herbs and spices indoors with bowls of homemade potpourri. This, by the way, bears no visual or perfumed resemblance to the synthetic stuff in discount stores.

Potpourri (literally, 'rotten pot') ingredients are dried and preserved using a fixative such as orris root, which allows them to release their fragrance into the air. Medieval housewives liked theirs wet and soggy, and kept it in jars with perforated lids, but unless you are keen on period re-enactments, the dried method is much more appealing.

A simple summer potpourri

(see page 150)

Collect flowers and herbs in summer. Make sure they are dry and free from bugs. You can remove the petals and leaves from the stems, or not. I prefer small rosebuds, which dry in an attractive way, rather than large blooms.

rose petals
miniature rose buds
lavender flowers
½ tsp powdered orris root
2–3 drops of essential rose oil

Place the flowers on newspaper or kitchen paper, and keep in a warm place for a few days. You can also dry them in the microwave: experiment with settings, but 2 minutes on high should work. They are ready to use when dry and brittle. If you're collecting over the summer, store what you've already prepared in a cool, dark place until you're ready to assemble the whole lot.

A pot pourri for Christmas:

rose petals
rosemary
dried orange or lemon
 peel
chopped ginger
allspice
allspice oil.

Then it's simply a matter of putting the dried material in a bowl, sprinkling over the powdered orris root and drops of essential oil, and stirring gently with a wooden spoon or salad servers.

Leave to mature for a couple of weeks, in a dark place, then put in whatever bowl or container you fancy.

Pressing flowers

You don't need a fancy flower press to press flowers – a heavy book or a telephone directory will do. If using a book with printed pages, put the flowers and leaves between pieces of clean kitchen or tissue paper. There's a lot of moisture in flowers and they may pick up the ink. Don't use kitchen paper with heavy embossing as this won't allow the flowers to lie completely flat.

Simple pressed summer flowers

(see page 153)

Collect the flowers when they're in full bloom but haven't begun to fade. Don't collect them early in the morning or after a downpour. Keep the stems and leaves on or remove them, as you wish; it depends on how thick they are and how you want the finished page in your album to look. You can even press the root if it isn't too thick.

flowers, herbs, weeds, grasses etc
album with blank, acid-free paper pages
flower press – telephone directory or heavy book
kitchen or tissue paper
white all-purpose glue
small paintbrush

Open the book at the middle and lay the material to be pressed on the clean paper. Arrange the petals and leaves exactly as you want them to appear when pressed; don't overcrowd them. You can press several pages of flowers at the same time.

Close the book and place on top as many heavy books, or something similar in weight (I use a cast iron griddle), as is necessary to make the press as flat as possible. Leave it closed for about a week.

Mounting the dried material: Open the book very carefully; the flowers are now dry and delicate.

Mount them in your album using clear glue. Do this by placing the flower or leaf (underside uppermost) on a piece of kitchen paper or clean newspaper. Use a paintbrush to apply a light but even layer of glue to the underside, brushing really gently.

Place right-side-up on the album page, cover with another piece of clean paper, and gently press the specimen to make sure the glue is evenly distributed. Use a piece of clean kitchen paper to wipe off any excess.

NOTES FROM MY SUMMER GARDEN

Bees in decline
We need bees to
pollinate flowers and
make honey. But with
the global bee
population in a
catastrophic decline,
in a syndrome known as
'Colony Collapse
Disorder', they must be
encouraged and given as
many bee-friendly
flowers as possible on
which to do their stuff.

The air is thick with the smell of damp grass and there's a whiff of the peppery nasturtiums, all scarlet and orange flowers, that have seeded themselves between the courgettes, radish rows and wigwams of beans. I welcome them for their unruly splashes of bright colour and because they help to deter pests.

The runner beans (see opposite) coil around the twiggy willow supports, curling skywards, and are heavy with the first batch of dangling pods, sweet and ready to pick. When the dog trots in from the garden and I tickle her velvety ear, my hands smell of the sweet lavender that she has skittered past on her way to see off the fox, next door's cat, or some other specimen of suburban wildlife.

Bee-friendly flowers:

foxglove
globe artichoke
globe thistle
sunflower
bluebell
wallflower
white dead-nettle
mint
rosemary
lemon balm
thyme
zinnia
lavender
honeysuckle
chives

After this week's torrential downpours there's little that can hold back the battalions of snails lurking in the dripping leafy undergrowth. My best efforts lie with sunken plastic cups filled with beer into which the slimy beasts are lured. Away, too, from their designs on the sweet leaves of the peas, whose pods are also nicely plump.

And despite some silvery telltale snail trails across their spreading foliage, the courgettes are budding, yellow, fat and glossy. Together with the ripening crop of cherry tomatoes, I am giving them copious drinks of water mixed with my sister-in-law's comfrey fertilizer (see Tomatoes, page 33). Starting off demurely in leafy rows, the rocket has gone into freefall, brimming over the vegetable patch's wooden enclosure with yellow flowers, which will go to seed if I don't pick them out now.

The basil loves the steamy warm air and has grown voluptuous green scented leaves; I need to pick it ruthlessly to avoid that going to seed too. I needn't worry about the bushy potato plants flowering though; because their plump tubers nestling in the earth will be filling and growing and ready to dig up in a couple of

**More allies
in the garden:**

Birds feed on grubs,
caterpillars, slugs and
aphids.

Frogs and toads are
predators of slugs,
woodlice and
small insects.

Ladybirds, hoverflies
and lacewings feed
on aphids.

Ground insects such as
spiders and centipedes
feed on insect pests.

weeks. Even if the summer garden isn't quite the riot of colour that it was in June, when the first vigorous flush of rose blooms erupted in a mass of pinks and whites, there are starburst-shaped agapanthus to enjoy in the large terracotta pots, each swaying flower head almost impossibly supported on a slender green stem, heavy with trumpet-shaped petals in everything from the palest lavender to the darker mauvy colours.

And there are enough roses making a second appearance – Eglantine and Gertrude Jekyll – not to feel downhearted. The fuzzy balls of purple globe thistles give height and colour to the borders, and attract bees and pairs of fluttering painted lady butterflies.

And I am almost forgetting the sweet peas, trailing up the metal arches to pour out flower after scented flower in pale lilacs and pinks. Cutting them daily for the table, or for the bathroom or the office, is the secret to repeat flowering.

Summer garden tasks

**DIY remedies for
bites and stings:**

Ease pain,
inflammation, itching
and swelling with a bag
of frozen peas or
crushed ice in a plastic
bag, wrapped in a towel.

Reduce swelling by
rubbing with a cut
onion.

Relieve swelling by
dabbing the bite with a
blob of toothpaste: the
peppermint has a
cooling effect.

Lift the yellowing leaves of spring bulbs. Place the bulbs in shallow boxes and when dry, remove dead leaves, roots and skins, and store in a cool dry shed or room.

Deadhead the roses and sweet peas: as this will promote new blooms. Feed the roses after the first flush of blooms and remove sucker shoots.

Trim and pinch out the flowers from the tops of herbs that you do not want to go to seed, such as basil and coriander.

Control weeds among the vegetables and herbs by frequent hoeing.

Apply a mulch of compost or manure to hold in moisture for water-loving vegetables such as beans, cabbages or chard.

Watering in dry spells is vital. Water container-grown plants at least once a day – in the evening when it's cooler is best. Dress with damp peat if daily watering is impossible.

Feed tomatoes, beans and courgettes when the fruit are developing.

Sunburn and minor burns:

Nurture an Aloe Vera plant on the window sill and cut out the gel from inside the stem to treat mild sunburn.

Grate a potato and apply on the burned area.

Minor kitchen burns, such as those on fingers, can be immersed in a glass of ice water for 15-minute periods.

To make the plants more fruitful, pinch side shoots from tomatoes when they are 2.5cm (1¼ inches) long.

The more you pick of your beans and courgettes, the more you will get. If these plants are not picked regularly they will stop producing pods or turn into marrows.

Sow seeds for winter radishes and early winter lettuces.

Lift and store shallots, garlic and onions. When the tops are yellowing and bending over, ease the clusters of bulbs out of the ground with a fork, removing the soil and spreading the bulbs out to dry; turn every day or two, and cover if it rains. When dry, separate the bulb clusters, rub off the loose skins and store in a box or paper bag in a cool, dry room.

Cut lavender stalks just before the flowers are fully open. Tie in small loose bundles and hang in a warm shed or room to dry.

Take cuttings of bay, mint, rosemary, lavender and sage and insert in sandy soil in open ground, or in a pot filled with sand. Protect from the sun and wind.

Interplanting

It's worth looking at the possibilities of interplanting as it is a natural way to deter pests. Here are some well known combinations:

Marigolds

These have vivid orange flowers, and the scent of their leaves repels a variety of vegetable pests. Try interplanting with cabbages or tomatoes.

Garlic

This has germicidal and fungicidal properties; planted between strawberries, next to roses and beneath trees, it can be effective against fungal diseases.

Carrots

Carrots interplanted with onions help to prevent both carrot and onion fly because each blocks the scent of the other and this confuses the pest.

Wormwood

The odour of wormwood (also known as absinthe) is repellent to many insects; it is traditionally planted near currant bushes to protect them.

Good things to eat in fall: chestnuts, field mushrooms, apples, plums, sloes, crab apples, blackberries, russet apples, pumpkins, pheasant.

fall

It's September. It's swallows flying south. It's suntan washing off in the bath. It's back to school. It's polished shoes, timetables and a brisk swim at the lido on a mellow Sunday morning. As my children get down to their books with a vigour only seen at the start of a new year, I, too, am enthused with ideas for colours, new spaces and what to plant in the garden. August under cloudless Algarve skies has filled me with positive thoughts.

FIELD MUSHROOMS
AND WOVEN BASKETS

'Season of mists and mellow fruitfulness!
Close bosom-friend of the maturing sun;
Conspiring with him how to load and bless
With fruit the vines that round the thatch-eaves run.'
John Keats, 'To Autumn'[10]

Camilo taught my children how to search for mushrooms in the cork oak and chestnut groves near our house in Spain. Wiry, sun-beaten and resourceful, like all the older villagers, Camilo was as much an artist as a natural forager, storing his tools on simple hooks and shelves and weaving beautiful baskets from olive sprigs.

A mushroom hunt

Mushrooms on toast

Fry a handful of sliced mushrooms – field, ceps or chanterelles – in a pan with a dollop of butter, a chopped garlic clove and a handful of chopped parsley. Cook for a few minutes, until just soft, and serve on toast. I like to use sourdough bread.

When the fall rains had turned the dry, burnt, summer grass to a faint fuzz of green, we'd set off, Camilo, the kids and I, with a couple of small dogs in tow. The ground rules: cut, don't rip, a mushroom out of the earth (you want it to come up again next year), and don't lick your fingers in case you've touched a poisonous one.

The baskets (plastic bags make fungi sweaty) were soon filled with field mushrooms, chanterelles, parasols and ceps (know as 'penny buns' and by Italians as 'porcini'). You could smell the earthy muskiness of the fungi in the damp air, even before you saw them. The parasols looked the most dramatic, spreading like fairy umbrellas under the gnarled oak trees. Prompting whoops of joy, the most prized fungi were caesar's mushrooms, their orangey caps poking up among the carpets of fallen chestnut leaves. Many local mushroom hunters would sell them to wholesalers, whose trucks then whisked them off to smart restaurants in Madrid and Barcelona.

Drying mushrooms

Ceps ('porcini' or 'penny buns') are my favourite mushrooms for drying because their flavour becomes more intense. I spread thin slices of fungi on sheets of greaseproof paper, as if drying flowers for potpourri (see page 154), and leave them for a couple of days, turning regularly. Alternatively, I put them in a very, very low oven for some hours, on greaseproof-lined trays, also turning regularly. When cool, I pack them into screw-top jars, and use them in soups, stews and risottos for a lovely, woody mushroom flavour.

Back at home in England, we gather a basket of parasols on a warm fall afternoon, walking in ancient Berkshire parkland near my father-in-law's home. They're tasty, almost meaty, fried in a little butter with parsley – but as with all edible mushrooms, you shouldn't eat them in large quantities because they are difficult to digest.

And in London I can even find 'penny buns' in Brockwell Park on early, dewy morning dog walks (they pop up overnight, as fungi so mysteriously do, within the rich leafy humus under the evergreen oaks). On one occasion, the dog was barking madly at a hippy with grey flowing locks tied in a bandana. Apologies for my noisy mutt were followed by his offer of a mind-altering experience with the tiny toadstools or 'magic mushrooms' that he was gathering in the thick grass. Being a conscientious mother of three, of course I decline.

Don't wash wild mushrooms, just brush off the dirt and bugs – needless to say, there are special brushes for mushroom fanciers, but a toothbrush will do.

Mushroom risotto

serves 6

If you want to enjoy the mushroom experience all year round I'd recommend buying packets of dried porcini, which can be easily hydrated and added to soups, stews and risottos.

1½ tbsp extra virgin olive oil
75g/3oz/¾ stick butter
1 onion, finely chopped
2 garlic cloves, chopped
300g/10oz/scant 1½ cups risotto rice
1.2 litres/2 pints/5 cups hot chicken or vegetable stock (including the water the mushrooms have been rehydrated in)
200g/7oz/2 cups fresh mushrooms, sliced and fried for a few minutes with 25g/1oz/¼ stick butter and 1 garlic clove, chopped
50g/2oz/⅓ cup dried porcini mushrooms, rehydrated in a cup of warm water
3 tbsp cream
handful of parsley, roughly chopped
50g/2oz/½ cup grated Parmesan cheese
salt and freshly ground black pepper

Follow the recipe for risotto on page 10 but omit the green vegetables and herbs, and add the mushrooms a few minutes before the end of the rice cooking time.

Stir in the cream, parsley and Parmesan just before serving, and season to taste.

Mushroom and chestnut stuffing

enough for a 10kg/20lb bird

If we have a bird at Christmas or a large family gathering, we make this really tasty stuffing with the fruits of fall.

5 bacon rashers, roughly chopped
2 garlic cloves, roughly chopped
l large onion, roughly chopped
l apple, roughly chopped
100g/3½oz/⅔ cup dried figs, roughly chopped
2 tbsp dried porcini mushrooms, soaked in warm water and roughly chopped
grated rind of l lemon
400g/13oz/2½ cups cooked peeled chestnuts, roughly chopped
200g/7oz/3½ cups breadcrumbs from several-days-old bread
1 large egg, beaten
salt and freshly ground black pepper

In a pan, fry the bacon, garlic, onion, apple, figs, mushrooms and grated lemon rind on a medium heat for about 10 minutes. Add the chestnuts, breadcrumbs and beaten egg and mix thoroughly. Add a little water if the mixture is too dry. Now stuff and cook the bird according to your recipe's instructions. Before serving, make sure the stuffing is cooked all the way through.

Mushroom health and safety

It goes without saying that you can get very, very sick, or even die, from ingesting a poisonous mushroom. Always consult an expert or a very good photographic reference. My mushroom mentors are Roger Phillips, whose brilliant illustrated book *Mushrooms and Other Fungi of Great Britain and Europe* should be in every forager's library, and Antonio Carluccio, who is the king of how to pick and cook wild fungi.

'A' IS FOR APPLES

There's buckets of apple lore, from the Romans who prized apples more highly than figs, to Elizabethan lovers who exchanged 'love apples' (a woman would keep a peeled apple in her armpit until saturated with her sweat and give it to her lover to inhale).

Bring home a bag of crisp, crunchy apples, ideal fast food to eat raw anytime. Don't peel them. The skin contains fragrance, fibre and almost half of the apple's vitamin C content. Look out for old-fashioned varieties, such as St Edmund's Pippin, Maid of Kent, Kidd's Orange, Winter Pearmain and Cornish Honey Pin, which are grown around the country at specialist apple farms.

Some recommended apple varieties

Cooking apples:
Bramley's Seedlings
Golden Noble
Grenadier
Monarch

Dessert apples:
Cox's Orange Pippin
St Edmund's Pippin
James Grieve
Orleans Reinette

Even if they're just plain old supermarket Granny Smiths, a bowl of green apples makes a simple and pleasing decoration on the table. If you want a more unusual appearance and flavour, russets are wonderfully organic and old-fashioned looking. Their rough orange-brown skin belies a beautiful sweet flavour. Eat with a strong Cheddar or Spanish Manchego cheese instead of a pudding, or for a quick lunch/snack.

In September, the apple tree at the bottom of the garden swelled with big fat green Bramley cooking apples. My mother wrapped them individually in newspaper and stored them in a box in the attic. They have to be absolutely sound, for even a small break or bruise releases enzymes that hasten decay. The storage place has to be dry and cool and the apples cannot touch each other.

When we heard the attic ladder being yanked down, we knew that pudding that day would be baked apples swimming in a pool of raisins and delicious caramel-tasting sauce.

Baked apples

1 apple per person

Core each apple and cut a slit, as if to halve it, around the circumference. Place in an ovenproof dish or tin and stuff the centre of the cored apple with an equal mix of raisins and chopped walnuts, plus a dessertspoonful of muscovado sugar (a much richer taste than white) and a large knob of butter.

Place in an oven preheated to 150°C/300°F/Gas Mark 2, for about 30 minutes, until the apple is soft and the top is brown and caramelized.

Apple and ginger pudding

serves 6

I make this for practically every Sunday lunch in fall and winter – it is delicious with its syrupy ginger flavours. It looks beautiful and is quite easy to make.

for the syrup
4 cooking or large eating apples
juice of 1 lemon
90g/3¼oz/scant 1 stick butter
90g/3¼oz/scant ½ cup sugar
4 tbsp syrup from a jar of preserved ginger

for the cake
125g/4oz/1 stick butter, softened
125g/4oz/⅔ cup caster sugar
2 large eggs, beaten
125g/4oz/scant 1 cup self-raising flour
4 knobs preserved ginger, chopped

Peel, core and slice the apples and turn them in lemon juice to stop them going brown. Melt the butter in a saucepan. Add the sugar and syrup and stir until creamy and a pale toffee colour. Arrange the apple slices neatly in a greased 1kg (2lb) bread tin or 23cm (9 inch) cake tin. I line mine with greaseproof paper, which I grease again to be safe. Pour in the syrup mixture.

For the cake (which is based on the sponge recipe on page 151): Cream the butter and sugar together until pale and fluffy, beat in the eggs, and fold in the flour with a metal spoon. Stir in the chopped ginger and spread the cake mixture evenly over the apples.

Place in a preheated oven, 190°C/375°F/Gas Mark 5, for about 45 minutes. If the top browns overly, reduce the heat.

Test for readiness with a skewer in the middle of the cake. It if comes out clean, without sticky cake mixture on it, it's done.

Cool the cake on a wire rack before turning out and peeling away the greaseproof paper. Eat with ice-cream, crème fraîche or blackberry sorbet (see page 179).

Apple pudding

serves 4

This is a more simple version of the recipe on the previous page.

After crossing sticks on the muddy hockey field by the river in Barnes, legs pink and chafed because of the rough prewar-style purple culottes we had to wear, I really looked forward to my mum's sweet and comforting apple pudding.

4 large apples
50g/2oz/¼ cup caster sugar (optional)
100g/3½oz/scant 1 stick butter
100g/3½oz/1 cup golden syrup
1 large egg, beaten
100g/3½oz/¾cup self-raising flour

Peel, core and slice the apples and arrange them in the bottom of a pie dish (if using cooking apples, counter their sourness by adding the caster sugar).

Melt the butter and syrup in a saucepan. Remove from the heat and cool before adding the well-beaten egg and beating together to a light thick cream. Fold in the flour gradually with a metal spoon. Spread the mixture over the fruit and place in an oven preheated to 200°C/400°F/Gas Mark 6, for 30 minutes.

This is really good with anything cold and creamy: vanilla ice cream, crème fraîche or fromage frais.

Apple crumble

serve 4–6

Preparing apples
A squeeze of lemon juice stops the raw apple slices from going brown.

My garden has a glorious old apple tree. In spring, it is a mass of pink, papery blossom. We sit under its cool shade in summer. I pick its greeny-gold fruit in September and think about how, when its new roots were settling, the skies were empty of vapour trails, and horses' hooves clattered on the road outside. Now that the tree is leaning with the weight of the years, I have propped up its main arm with a wooden pole, like tucking a hand under the elbow of an elderly relative.

Apple crumble is an easy and delicious way to work through an apple glut. It combines the health factor of fruit with the buttery, sweet and fill-you-up-quickly appeal of the crumble.

Peel, core and slice 4 large cooking apples. Place at the bottom of a 1 litre (1¾ pint) dish. (If you've been blackberrying, throw in a couple of generous handfuls for the vibrant pink juices of blackberry and apple crumble.)

Prepare the crumble as in the recipe for Rhubarb crumble on page 59. Spread it on top of the apples and add a handful of flaked almonds and a couple of tablespoons of brown sugar if you want more texture and sweetness.

Place the whole lot in an oven preheated to 180°C/350°F/Gas Mark 4, for 40–45 minutes. Serve hot (cold apple crumble doesn't really do it for me), especially with thick cream or dollops of vanilla ice-cream.

Apple purée

One way to use up sad, withered or bruised apple specimens in the fruit bowl is to magic them into a purée. This is also a good way of dealing with the bland supermarket offerings that might be the only apples you can get hold of in winter.

It's just the sort of easy-to-get-down, nutritious food you can persuade a fussy child to eat (babies, in my experience, need no encouragement). Make a big batch and freeze it in small tubs or plastic bags.

Use purée too for serving with roast pork or as a pudding with yogurt or cream.

Peel, core and slice 4 large apples and cook them in a pan with a little water, a squeeze of lemon juice and a teaspoon of cinnamon. When the apples are soft, blend with a whizzer until smooth. Sweeten with honey.

FALLEN FRUIT

You don't have to be a country bumpkin to go fruit picking. It's amazing how many fruity treasures, from quinces to crab apples, hang over fences and public walls in cities and urban spaces.

The other day, for example, I read about a clever initiative in Los Angeles called Fallen Fruit. The three instigators are all keen gardeners and noticed a prevalence of fruit and nut trees in their neighbourhood, including avocados, walnuts, plums, apricots, almonds, oranges, lemons and limes. Many had branches that extended over their fences, from private into public space. The group now organizes Nocturnal Fruit Foraging events, where crowds of up to 80 people roam the streets, gathering fruit and nuts in shopping trolleys. They organize Public Fruit Jams, where people turn their pickings into jams, and they distribute fruit trees so that people can plant more. Where trees once had fruit rotting on their branches, they are now picked bare.

Fallen Fruit has led to the discovery of fruity surprises, such as finding the fringes of the No. 5 Freeway thick with pomegranates, or the 101 lined, for no discernible reason, with avocado trees. And old citrus trees are now reasserting themselves in gardens all over LA.

Crab apple jelly

makes 4-6 x 250g (8oz) jars

I am definitely a follower of the Fallen Fruit philosophy. Top of my list for local foraging are crab apples – living ancestors of the cultivated apple. The council has obligingly planted a scattering of these trees on the route to my children's school.

The little apple-shaped yellow fruits (see opposite) drop and lie squashed and wasted on the pavement unless someone like me comes along and scoops them up to make a divine pink, scented jelly to eat with roast lamb or simply on toast for tea.

2kg/4lb crab apples
about 500g/1lb/2½ cups granulated sugar

Wash and chop the crab apples and put them in a pan with enough water just to cover them. Bring slowly to the boil, then simmer gently until soft. Stir occasionally and mash the apples once or twice with a potato masher to really break them up and extract the pectin.

Ladle the fruit and juice into a bag made from muslin (place a large square of muslin across a bowl, lay the fruit in the middle and gather up the sides with string). I hang this bag from a hook on the rail above my sink and allow the juice to drip into the bowl for several hours.

Pour the strained juice back into the pan and add the sugar. As a guide, use 500g/1lb sugar per 500ml/17fl oz of extracted juice. Stir over a low heat to dissolve the sugar and then bring to the boil. Boil rapidly, stirring all the time, until setting point is reached. This takes about 20 minutes. The jelly is set if a teaspoonful wrinkles when pushed with a spoon on an ice-cold plate (see page 178). When ready, pot in jars that have been washed thoroughly and sterilized in a hot oven for a few minutes.

General points for jam and jelly making

Choose ripe or just-ripe fruit. Certain fruits have a high setting quality, so they set more quickly than others. Some fruits, such as strawberries and apricots, require the addition of lemon juice, high in pectin and acid, to set properly. Some fruits are juicier than others and require less water. All the fruits mentioned here are high in pectin and shouldn't need lemon juice to set.

Make the following jellies using the same method and proportions of fruit, sugar and water as for the crab apple jelly on the previous page.

Gooseberry and mint jelly: You don't need to top and tail the berries. Add a handful of crushed mint leaves to the jelly bag.

Quince jelly: Cut the quinces into thick chunks for quicker cooking. Choose firm fruits or just under-ripe for a better set.

Redcurrant jelly: Cook them, stalks and all, in the pan. Do the same with blackcurrants.

If all fails, and the jellies don't set as well as you'd like, just use them as delicious sauces for meat or for pouring over ice-cream.

Another way to rescue unset jellies, albeit rather laborious, is to pour the whole lot back in the pan and add extra lemon juice, reboil until it reaches setting point, cool and re-pot.

To test for setting:
Take a teaspoon of the jelly and put it on an ice-cold saucer to cool quickly. Prod with a finger and, if the skin wrinkles, the jelly is cooked sufficiently. If it remains smooth, cook for a further 5–10 minutes, then repeat the test. This test also works for jam.

Blackberries

In between shopping and loading up the bike pannier, I picked enough blackberries for a crumble, by the car park fence where overhanging brambles from neighbouring wasteland are heavily laden with glossy fruit. Staining fingers with their deep pink juice, the colour of some exotic paint, blackberries make gorgeously deep fuchsia-pink sorbet, blackberry and apple crumble or jam.

Blackberry and apple jam
makes 4-6 x 250g (8oz) jars

1kg/2lb/8 cups blackberries
125ml/4fl oz/½ cup water
350g/11½oz apples (sour ones such as Bramleys have higher levels of pectin)
caster sugar

Stew the blackberries in half the water until tender, 5 minutes or so. Sieve, if you want seedless jam. As with the sorbet below, I don't mind the seeds. Peel, core and slice the apples and stew until tender in the remaining water. Add to the blackberries. Weigh and add an equal amount of sugar. Stir until dissolved, bring to the boil and test for setting. Pour into warmed jars and cover with a waxed paper disc.

Blackberry sorbet

serves 4

100g/3½ oz/½ cup caster sugar
100ml/3½fl oz/½ cup water
500g/1lb/4 cups blackberries
1 egg white

Make a syrup by boiling the sugar and water for 4 minutes. Cool. Push the berries through a sieve if you don't want the pips, or pulverize them with a hand-held blender (I do the latter as I don't mind pips). Mix the fruit mush with the syrup. Beat the egg white until it forms soft peaks and fold it into the mixture. Put it in a freezer-proof dish (I use an old ice-cream container), cover and freeze to a mush. Stir and freeze for a further 30 minutes. Stir again and freeze until set: allow another couple of hours.

Plum tart

serves 6–8

Plums fresh from the tree simply melt in the mouth with sweetness. Oval-shaped Victoria plums with glossy purple skins are an old favourite in many suburban back gardens and farmers' markets brim with many different choices. Anna Spath and Coe's Golden Drop are just two varieties found in specialist orchards at this time of year.

Even if the margins for error for pastry (a temperamental thing) are less than those for a crumble, a homemade tart with glazed whirls of fruit is a little work of art that will be appreciated at the table. Use ready-made pastry or make your own.

I recently came upon Angela Boggiano's book *Pie₁₁*, in which her mantra for making good pastry is handle it lightly, keep it cool and bake it in a hot oven.

Pastry tips:

Hands should be cool.

Chill pastry in the fridge before cooking.

Handle the pastry lightly.

Rub the butter into the flour with your fingertips rather than using a food processor.

Roll out using gentle strokes between two sheets of greaseproof paper to stop it sticking.

Bake in a hot oven.

To avoid pastry with a soggy bottom, heat a baking sheet in a hot oven for about 15 minutes, then sit the tart tin on the sheet to bake – this will ensure a crispy bottom.

Don't use too thick a dish – the oven may not be hot enough – and don't put too high in the oven or cook too quickly.

for rich sweet pastry
200g/7oz/1½ cups plain flour
pinch of salt
100g/3½oz/scant 1 stick unsalted butter, chilled and cut into small pieces
50g/2oz/¼ cup caster sugar
1 tsp lemon juice
1 large egg, beaten
or **300g/10oz ready-made sweet pastry, chilled**

for the filling
600g/1¼lb plums (green ones, golden ones, Victorias, whatever you can lay your hands on)
2 tbsp caster sugar
3 tbsp blackcurrant jam (or plum, apricot, strawberry, whatever you've got in the cupboard)
1 tbsp cassis

Sift the flour and salt into a bowl and rub in the butter. Add the sugar and lemon juice and then the egg. Mix and mould into a ball with your fingertips. Turn out and knead for a few minutes, until smooth.

Roll out the pastry into a circle on a floured surface, about the thickness of a one-pound coin (3mm/⅛ inch), and line either a 23cm (9 inch) shallow pie tin that you can serve from, or a greased 23cm (9 inch) loose-bottomed tart tin if you want to transfer the tart easily to a plate.

Ease the pastry into the tin without stretching. Roll over the top with a rolling pin to cut off any surplus pastry. Leave the edge plain or flute it with a knife or fork. Chill in the fridge for 30 minutes.

Place a baking sheet in an oven preheated to 190°C/375°F/Gas Mark 5. Prick the base of the pastry with a fork, line with foil, and weigh down with dried beans. Bake on the hot baking sheet for 10 minutes, then take it out and remove the beans and paper. Increase the oven temperature to 200°C/ 400°F/Gas Mark 6.

More tart ideas
Slices of peeled apple or pear, peaches or apricots makes an equally delicious tart.

Halve and stone the plums, then cut them into thin slices. Sprinkle the base of the semi-cooked pastry evenly with half the sugar and arrange the plums in concentric circles. Pack them in as tightly as possible, but try not to overlap. Sprinkle with the rest of the sugar and bake for 15 minutes.

Turn down the heat to 190°C/375°F/Gas Mark 5 and cook for a further 10–15 minutes, until the pastry is nicely brown.

While the tart is cooking, put the jam and cassis in a pan and simmer for a few minutes. Let the tart cool, then brush with the glaze. Serve cold or warm.

Quince paste or *membrillo*

Foodie heaven on a budget? I suggest a few quinces, the golden apples of mythology, made into quince paste or *membrillo*, as it is called in Spain. More like a jelly than a paste, eat these sweet-but-tart slices (I add lemon juice) with a strong cheese such as Manchego. Quinces require a bit of sleuthing to track down. Fall is

the season for quinces. I have often loaded a suitcase with an armload picked from the *finca* in Andalucia, where quince trees grow prolifically.

A surprising number of English country gardens possess the quince, so ask around. This year I struck lucky with beautiful plump and golden specimens from a neighbourhood tree on sale in a wooden box at a local greengrocer. And they're the kind of unusual garden produce that will sometimes turn up at farmers' markets. If you are planting a quince tree, site it near water if you can, as quinces love water.

Quince paste

(Quince paste and Manchego)

It's a lovely idea to bring out *membrillo* at Christmas (or at any other time when you want to serve a special pudding, or even just enjoy it as a tapa or snack). Cut it in slivers and serve with Manchego or hard cheese, and a little glass of something sweet such as muscatel wine. Wrapped in some nice waxed paper and tied with a ribbon, homemade *membrillo* is a lovely idea for a Christmas gift.

3kg/6lb quinces
sugar
juice of 2 lemons

Cut up the quinces – peel, pips, core and all. Put them in a deep, heavy based saucepan, cover with water and simmer until soft. Purée the mixture with a hand-held blender and weigh it, adding an equal amount of sugar plus the juice of 2 lemons (for flavour rather than their setting qualities).

Simmer the mixture, stirring constantly, until it turns a rich red colour. Line shallow trays with greaseproof paper and spread the hot paste about 4cm (1½ inches) deep. Leave to dry and harden in a cool place. I divide the slabs of paste into paperback book-sized pieces, wrap them in greaseproof paper, and store them in a tin until needed.

RIPE FOR ROASTING

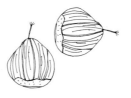

On smoky fall afternoons, wearing matching duffle coats, ribbed tights and gloves, my sister and I would race around looking for fallen chestnuts under the ancient sweet chestnut trees in Richmond Park. My mum would later score and grill them in a metal pan and split them open for us, revealing the steaming, sweet, floury and potato-like insides.

I really got to know my chestnuts when we went to live among the leafy groves in the Sierra hills of Andalucia. It was here that my husband set up a little factory processing the local crop.

Cooking and peeling chestnuts

Peeling chestnuts is a laborious but unavoidable task. This is the best way to do it:

Use a sharp knife to make an incision through the shell just into the flesh and work your way almost around the nut's circumference. Now roast the chestnuts at 180°C/350°F/Gas Mark 4 for about 30 minutes. Wait until cool enough to hold, then remove each shell and papery inner skin.

The whole family quickly became conversant in chestnut facts and figures. We learnt that the spiky green pompoms, with their glossy brown nuts, fall from trees planted in neat avenues 500 years ago by natives of Castile and León, sent down to repopulate the area after the expulsion of the Moors. The *tempranas*, the early crop, falls in September, while the main harvest – the *tradias* – tumbles down from the trees from late October onward. Most of the chestnut farms are around 2 hectares (4–5 acres) in size and extended families get together to take part in the back-breaking business of chestnut-gathering.

The chestnut is rich in complex carbohydrates, very low in fat and high in vitamin C (it is the only nut to contain this vitamin). They are also a good source of fibre and have been a staple of the peasant diet for hundreds of years. They can be added to soups, roasted with meats or vegetables, candied, made into jam or dried and ground into flour.

Chestnuts remain a firm fixture on the list of things I like to cook. We roast the season's chestnuts over an open fire by slitting and tossing them among the hot embers for a few minutes. One year a friend gave me a chestnut roaster – a pan with slotted holes that you hold over the fire and jiggle the roasting nuts around in for about 5 minutes, until it is brown and soft on the inside. Leave the chestnuts to cool before peeling.

It's also good to buy bags of roasted chestnuts from steaming trolleys on cinema outings in London's West End, on chilly fall evenings.

In Olhão, you can buy chestnuts from an old man sporting a prewar cycle helmet who arrives with a rickety brazier towed on a piece of rope attached to a vintage motorbike. He folds cones of newspaper and stacks them ice-cream-cornet style beside the swirling smoke and cooking nuts. Or there is the wagon manned by two Romanies, where you can dip the roasted nuts in a rough wooden bowl of sea salt.

Chestnut, chorizo and tomato soup

serves 4–6

I use peeled chestnuts to make everything from soups to stuffing. This delicious, rich red soup, with chestnuts, chorizo and tomato, is just the thing to serve if you're having a bonfire party, or are going on a fall picnic. The chestnuts give bulk, texture and a subtle nutty taste and the *pimentón* creates a nice smoky quality and warms you up.

1kg/2lb tomatoes
2 tbsp extra virgin olive oil
1 onion, roughly chopped
3 garlic cloves, roughly chopped
1 tsp *pimentón*
200g/7oz/2 cups cooked and peeled chestnuts, roughly chopped
1 litre/1¾ pints/4 cups chicken stock (see page 235)
100g/3½oz chorizo (the sausage-shaped one, not the thin slices in
  vacuum packs), chopped into small pieces
handful of parsley or coriander, roughly chopped
salt and freshly ground black pepper

Pierce the tomatoes, then blanch them in boiling water for 1 minute. Remove the skins and chop the flesh roughly. Heat the olive oil in a pan and add the onion and garlic. Cook for a few minutes until soft, then add the tomatoes and *pimentón* and simmer for 5 minutes.

Add the chestnuts and simmer for a further 3 minutes. Pour in the stock and liquidize or purée in batches.

Return the soup to the pan, add the chorizo and simmer for a few minutes. Add the herbs, season to taste and serve.

Storing chestnuts

Fresh chestnuts are firm to the touch and heavy in the hand, with no space between the shell and the flesh. They are more perishable than other nuts, but can be stored for up to a month in a cool, dry place, or in a plastic bag in the crisper of your fridge.

SEW EASY

Work box essentials:

tape measure
dressmakers' chalk
scissors for cutting
  paper patterns and
  templates
embroidery scissors
  with short blades for
  trimming threads
rustproof dressmaking
  pins
sharp needles (canvas
  will require a thick one)
thimble
tacking thread
buttons
white and black thread
safety pins
steam iron for pressing
  hems and seams

When the clocks go back and darkness falls early, and there are no more bike rides or early evening walks with the dog in the park, there seems more time and fewer excuses not to get out my sewing box.

Just as I like to squeeze numerous inspirations from the leftover roast (see page 206), I've always been one of those girls who've cut off their old jeans for shorts, or shrunk a too-big top to make it look more clingy and sexy. My mum's waste-not-want-not ethic has a lot to do with it. As a teenager in the 1970s, if we wanted something new it wasn't a question of trotting off to Primark – we had to be a little more creative. I can appreciate this stout advice from a World War II Board of Trade *Make Do and Mend* leaflet:

'Cami-knickers that have gone at the top can be cut down into knickers. And those that have gone in the legs can be cut off just below the waist to make what used to be called a "chemise". You will find that a "chemise and knicker" set made from two old cami-knickers will give you a great deal more wear.'

Make and do

Extend the life of grungy sheets, or simply rather nasty avocado-coloured ones that a kind aunt has passed on to you, by dyeing them in your favourite colour. I am rather fond of little tins of Dylon in Ocean Blue, a lovely refreshing shade that can be used in the washing machine, a less mucky process than cold-dyeing items in the bath. Make an almost instant duvet cover by stitching two dyed white sheets together on three sides. Hem along the top opening, and stitch on ties made from lengths of cotton tape.

Patches and patchwork

Use patchwork to decorate a plain duvet cover – a simple band across the top or maybe a border all the way round. Mix large and small designs but stick to a theme, such as 1960s' geometrics, or pretty vintage florals. Jumble sales and charity shops are a great source of potential patchwork material.

If you're planning on adding patchwork to an existing duvet cover, unpick the side seams for easier handling. To make the pieces of patchwork, cut 22cm (9 inch) squares with 1cm (½ inch) seams and sew together in a row. Turn to the underside and stitch 1cm (½ inch) hems around the edges. Pin or tack the pieces of patchwork to the cover and stitch into place.

Even old blankets can be glammed up with an edging of velvet ribbon, and if they're just too grotty, you can use them as a layer of extra warmth and padding under the base sheet.

All bedrooms need a small armchair, with a pretty, loose chair cover. I would suggest some robust cream linen. Or you could customize an existing cover, which is what I did recently with a floral cover on which I stitched a bottom frill and patches to the arms and seat in blue and white ticking. A simple, homespun look.

Magic hems

Just as a bag of frozen peas works magic in the kitchen, iron-on hem tape is the equivalent in my sewing box, because it requires no sewing at all. I use it for turning up dresses, skirts, trousers, and hemming curtains, cushion covers, tablecloths etc.

To turn up a dress

Get a friend to help measure the hem level when you're trying on the garment. Stand on a table or chair so the fitter can see straight away the hang of the hem. Decide on the hem length. Turn up evenly all the way round, inserting pins to fix.

Decide on the hem width and trim the surplus to an even depth from the hem edge. Turn under a narrow first turning, to provide a neat edge. Press lightly. Place iron-on hem tape along the inside edge, fold over and press into place.

An easy repair

When a sheet begins to wear, take action before a small hole becomes a large one. Place a piece of tissue paper over the hole on the wrong side, then go back and forwards over the hole and paper with a sewing machine.

Turn the sheet to the right side and stitch across the hole. Wash the sheet normally and the paper will dissolve in the water, leaving a neat darn.

FLAPJACKS AND PUMPKINS

What goes around comes around. And here I am sitting around a pale wood Ercol table, drinking tea and eating gooey oat flapjacks – just as I did several decades back in my parents' house in south-west London. The thought, back then, of liking anything that my parents did was unthinkable, so uncool.

But after flying the nest, much of life seems to be spent connecting with the familiar and reassuring aspects of our childhood and then reliving it through our own children (for example, hot water bottles, ice-cream in cones, thick pyjamas). Even to the extent of choosing partners, who might look like and have similar temperaments to our parents, as one psychotherapist I spoke to suggested.

Through my work as a stylist and designer I have gained a degree of professional admiration for Ercol design. But it was more the rush of nostalgia (I remember my fifth birthday cake and tea, the day I let the dog walk on the table and the claw marks that sent my mother wild) that propelled my intensive searches on eBay for the simple elm stick-back Ercol chairs and tables that are now a 1950s design classic. One search led me to a garage in Bedfordshire and a set of Windsor table and chairs in fabulous condition. Even the flat tyre on the way home didn't dim my enthusiasm.

Flapjacks with a little lemony flavour

serves 4–6

Flapjacks are food classics that haven't needed a new generation to rediscover their sweet, comforting delights. They keep on appearing on the menu for tea. Just the thing to stop everyone dissolving into rattiness on one of those long walks over Dartmoor on visits to my grandmother in Devon at half-term.

Spoonfuls of golden syrup provide the chewy texture required in a properly made flapjack and the muscovado sugar gives them a richer toffee taste.

100g/3½oz/scant 1 stick butter
3 generous tbsp golden syrup
75g/3oz/scant ½ cup muscovado sugar
squeeze of lemon juice
225g/7½oz/2½ cups jumbo rolled oats

(see also recipe for Oat
biscuits on page 225)

Melt the butter, syrup and sugar in a pan. Add a squeeze of lemon juice. Stir in the oats, pack the mixture into a greased baking tray and cook in an oven preheated to 180°C/350°F/Gas Mark 4, for 30 minutes, until golden. Divide into squares or rectangles while still warm, then turn out onto a wire rack to cool completely.

It's Halloween!

October 31st is Halloween, All Hallows' Eve, and in keeping with all the spookery of the day's ritual, we carve a pumpkin that glows with an eerie leer when lit up with a tealight. The creamy sun-yellow flesh doesn't go to waste. I fry pieces in butter and garlic until soft and purée it with some Parmesan and cream to make a quick, colourful sauce for pasta or mix it with chicken stock for soup. Alternatively, I simply roast chunks of it in the oven with garlic and olive oil.

Apple bobbing and other games

Fill a bowl with water and apples, and see who can grab as many apples as they can by their mouth – no hands, or it's cheating. Try to do this outside because it makes a frightful wet mess. That's why children love it.

When the annual rerun of John Carpenter's film *Halloween* is on TV, I have to leave the room while Jamie Lee Curtis's teenage babysitter is being stalked by the traumatized boy-turned-bogeyman-killer.

My spooky story game is somewhat more tame. Sit the children blindfolded in a circle and, as part of the scary story you've made up, pass around objects from it such as the witches' eyes (grapes), rats' innards (spaghetti rings) and dead men's finger stew (sausages). Be as evil as you dare.

And build a bonfire. Bake potatoes in the embers (see opposite) and pass round mugs of hot soup – the Chestnut, chorizo and tomato recipe on page 186 is suitably smoky and rich for a dank fall night.

THE HUMBLE SPUD

Ways with potatoes:

Buy loose, unwashed potatoes, as the soil helps to keep them fresh.

Mashed, roasted, baked and chipped potatoes require a floury variety: King Edward, Desiree, Fianna or Maris Piper.

Use waxy varieties for classic dauphinoise or salads: Wilja, Charlotte, Pink Fir Apple or Cara.

I cook new potatoes with a sprig of mint for flavour.

'There is too much talk of cooking being an art or a science – we are only making ourselves something to eat,' says my food hero, Nigel Slater, in his book *Real Cooking$_{12}$*. What a breath of fresh air this is to all of us home cooks. He's not saying that we shouldn't bother with our food, but – rather than get all technical and rarefied – we should enjoy cooking for its own sake. I like to think that the recipes in this book echo his philosophy.

Take the humble baked potato, for example: crisp, earthy brown skin and fluffy steaming insides, combined with a spoonful or two of cream cheese and chopped green herbs. Pure luxury.

Baked spuds

If, like me, you prefer a salty crust, slash the potato with a cross and sprinkle with olive oil and rough grains of sea salt. Another delicious idea is to purée equal quantities of crème fraîche and petit pois, a handful of mint, and sea salt and freshly ground black pepper to serve as a topping (see page 194).

As well as making a quick lunch or supper if eaten on their own, hot baked spuds can be the cornerstone of a meal. I like to eat them with cold roast beef or chicken, or smoked salmon, a plate of cold shrimps or salad: no fancy preparations at all, other than maybe a bowl of alioli as an accompaniment (see page 101).

Stick a metal skewer through the middle of each potato to ensure it gets a fluffy middle and cooks more quickly.

Thinking ahead is the success to the baked potato. Allow an hour or so for a large potato to cook in a hot oven, 200°C/400°F/Gas Mark 6. Like soggy pastry, an under-cooked spud is grim.

Mash

The most important elements for creamy, fluffy mashed potato are – apart from the spuds themselves – a simple hand potato masher, cream and butter. There's a fashion for loosely mashing potatoes with their skins on, which is jolly delicious, but I can't get enough of a basic creamy mash to eat with meat, fish and other vegetables, or to incorporate into Shepherd's pie (see page 229), fish pie, fish cakes, bubble and squeak (see page 232), or the fried mashed potato dish, hash browns.

Chopped spring onions added to mashed potato makes Irish champ. Alternatively, add a few filaments of saffron (see page 134) that have been infused in hot water to give mashed potato an aromatic flavour and a rich yellow colour.

Peel or leave the skins on, whichever you prefer, and put in enough boiling salted water to cover. Put a lid on the pan and boil the potatoes gently. (Rapid boiling makes them break and become mushy.)

When tender, drain and shake over a low heat for a minute or 2 to make them dry and floury. The secret of mashing is a vigorous pulverizing for several minutes (hard work, but worth it), followed by a bit of forking to loosen any really stubborn lumps.

Roast spuds

serves 4–6, depending on how many teenage boys are at the table

Reams of debate about what makes the perfect roast potato go on in the kitchens of the land.

My benchmark is simple, whether the 16-year-old approves or not. I am warned before every meal involving roast potatoes that they must be very crispy.

The key is parboiling before you throw the spuds in the oven with the temperature set high and the fat hot. Here again, the type of fat provides more room for debate. The Nigella effect, prompted by the TV cook's enthusiasm for goose fat in her Christmas episode, caused jars of the stuff to fly off supermarket shelves. I think that potatoes roasted in olive oil are as delicious as anything.

1kg/2lb floury potatoes (King Edward, for example), peeled
6 tbsp extra virgin olive oil
sea salt

Cut the potatoes into equal-sized chunks and parboil in a pan of salted boiling water for 7–10 minutes. While they are cooking, heat the oil in a roasting pan in an oven preheated to 180°C/350°F/Gas Mark 4. When hot, add the drained potatoes and toss in the hot oil until coated. Roast for 40–60 minutes, basting every 10 minutes or so.

If roasting a piece of meat, put the potatoes around it in the same pan to cook in the meat's fat, basting regularly.

**Potato wedges
with rosemary
and garlic**

Cut unpeeled potatoes into wedges and roast with olive oil, garlic, rosemary and sea salt in an oven preheated to 180°C/350°F/Gas Mark 4, for about 45 minutes.

**Gratin
dauphinois**

serves 6

When the chef had been at the brandy, it was up to the waiting staff to manage the cooking at the north London restaurant that I worked in to supplement my income in my first job as deputy beauty editor. Along with deep-fried Camembert with gooseberry sauce (1980s' bistro chic), I became rather good at gratin dauphinois potatoes. A timeless classic to eat with everything from a roast to a winter stew (see page 233).

1kg/2lb waxy potatoes (Charlotte, for example), thinly sliced
1 garlic clove, chopped
500ml/17fl oz/2 cups double cream
50g/2oz/½ stick unsalted butter
sea salt and freshly ground black pepper
Parmesan cheese (optional)

Arrange the potatoes in layers in a shallow dish; an earthenware one is traditional. Season with the garlic, salt and pepper. Pour the cream over the potatoes and dot the butter on top. Place in an oven preheated to 150°C/300°F/Gas Mark 2, for about 1¼ hours, until soft below and crispy on top.

Make sure the potatoes are cut thinly (too thick and they'll take too long) and be generous with the cream. Grated Parmesan on the top is a delicious variation.

Bonfire potatoes

Prick the potatoes with a fork, wrap them in foil and bury them in the embers of a firework party bonfire or a campfire. Leave to cook for an hour or two, depending on the heat of the ashes.

Open the foil, make a slit in the potato and add a blob of butter. It brings out the smoky flavour. Small people might need gloves to handle a hot potato.

BREAD

'The aesthetics of cooking applies as much, if not more, to food made out of simple ingredients such as flour and yeast, as it does to expensive ones.'
John Lane, *Timeless Simplicity*[13]

There's something so elemental about a piping hot loaf of homemade bread straight from the oven. Then there's the simple pleasure of making the bread itself. Kneading a springy, yielding piece of dough is contentment itself – a productive and calming kitchen workout that in its way is as satisfying as a trip to the gym.

Don't put the bread away until it is completely cool. I store mine in a 1940s green and cream enamelled metal bread bin I found on an early Sunday morning hunt around the market.

**Very easy
walnut bread**

makes 2 loaves

The olive oil in this recipe helps the crust go nice and brown. Substitute the walnuts for olives if you prefer, or make a mix of both: throw in some chopped rosemary or basil for added herby flavour.

500g/1lb/3½ cups strong white flour
2 tsp sea salt
1 tsp sugar
1 tbsp extra virgin olive oil
1½ tsp dried yeast
100g/3½oz/1 cup chopped walnuts
400ml/14fl oz/1¾ cups tepid water

In a warm bowl, mix the flour, sea salt, sugar, extra virgin olive oil, dried yeast and walnuts. Make a well in the centre, add the water and mix to a soft dough.

Turn it out onto a floured surface and knead for 10 minutes. Push it away from you with the palm of your hand, then fold it towards you and give a quarter turn. When the dough feels smooth and elastic, divide it into 2 rounds. Divide each round into 3 sausages and twist into plaits.

Put the 2 plaits of dough on to a greased baking sheet in a warm place, cover with a clean tea towel and leave for up to an hour or so, until doubled in size. Bake the loaves in the centre of an oven preheated to 230°C/450°F/Gas Mark 8, for 30–35 minutes, until brown on the outside.

Save money and bake several loaves in one session. Wrap and freeze the bread as soon as it has cooled. Thawed and warmed in the oven, it will taste as if it has been freshly made.

Variations

Another idea is to add a handful of seeds for a nutty texture: pumpkin, sesame, poppy, sunflower.

Seedy bread

Try this easy fibre-rich seed loaf containing omega-3 fatty acids. It is really more a cake than bread, since it is baked without yeast. This is my version of a recipe by nutrition guru Michael van Straten, torn out of the newspaper one wet Sunday afternoon.

Omega-3 fatty acids are billed as being good for the brain, protecting against heart disease and cancer and important during pregnancy for the proper formation of the baby's brain cells.

The best sources are: walnuts and linseed (flaxseed), some vegetable and nut oils (flax, walnut, rapeseed, soya bean, wheat germ) and oily fish (kippers, salmon, tuna).

For a sweeter version

For a sweeter version add 50g/2oz/¼ cup muscovado sugar.

200g/7oz/1¼ cups wholemeal flour
100g/3½oz/generous 1 cup porridge oats
50g/2oz/¼ cup linseed (flaxseed)
30g/1¼oz/¼ cup sunflower seeds
30g/1¼oz/¼ cup pumpkin seeds
3 tsp sesame seeds
3 tsp poppy seeds
1 tbsp grated lemon rind
20g/¾oz/⅛ cup grated fresh root ginger
200g/7oz/1¼ cups raisins
2 large eggs, beaten
300ml/½ pint/1¼ cups milk (skimmed, semi-skimmed or whole)
1 tbsp malt extract
75g/3oz/1 cup flaked almonds

Grease and line a 2lb (1kg) loaf tin or a round tin with greaseproof paper. Put all the ingredients except the almonds in a large bowl and mix thoroughly with a wooden spoon. If the mixture is too stiff, loosen it with a little more milk. Spoon the mixture into the tin, level off the surface with a knife and press the almonds into it. Place in an oven preheated to 190°C/375°F/Gas Mark 5, for about 1 hour. Stick a skewer in the middle to test whether it's ready – it will come out clean if it is.

Turn out and leave to cool. Spread with butter and jam, eat on its own or toast.

Easy peasy pizza
makes 4 pizzas

I went through a period of prickling at the word 'pizza'. It conjured up huge wasteful cardboard boxes containing dog-end pizza crusts from a mainly plastic-tasting substance, that one of the teenagers had ordered from a local takeout. My tastebuds were happily reactivated after going to Franco Manca's snug restaurant between the Rasta bonnets and packets of West African fufu flour in Brixton market. His glorious sourdough Italian pizzas made in a wood-fired oven are voted the best in Britain, no less.

Homemade pizza, made using basic bread dough and an ordinary oven, tastes delicious too. It's an inexpensive idea for parties, and a great way to get children cooking, because they can customize their own toppings.

500g/1lb/3½ cups strong white bread flour
1 tsp sea salt
1½ tsp dried yeast
1 tbsp extra virgin olive oil
300ml/¼ pint/1½ cups warm water

Cooking multiple pizzas

When there are several pizzas to cook for a family supper or party, I use the top rack of the oven but start some on the lower racks too, and as soon as the first one is done, whip the next one up to the top, and so on. I know this isn't ideal, but cooking one pizza at a time just takes too long.

Pizza needs a hot oven of 200°C/400°F/Gas Mark 6 to give it a crisp base. Put a flat baking sheet in the oven first to heat it up. The dough plus paper can slide straight on to the hot baking sheet. In this way, worktop and cooking surface are non-stick. Cooking takes about 20 minutes.

In a warm bowl, mix the flour, salt, dried yeast and oil. Make a well in the centre, add the water, and mix to a soft dough. Turn it out on a floured surface and knead for 10 minutes. When it feels smooth and elastic, put it back in the mixing bowl, cover with a tea towel and let it rest in a warm place for up to an hour, until it has doubled in size. Take it out and knock it back: punch lightly with your knuckles and let it rise again for 20 minutes.

Roll out into a sausage, divide into 4 pieces and roll into balls. Cut out 4 pieces of greaseproof paper the size of your baking sheets and flour lightly. Roll each piece of dough, the thinner the better, into rounds about 30cm (12 inches) in diameter. I don't mind them being irregular; it makes them more rustic, more authentic.

Some easy toppings

Cover the base with a thick layer of tomato sauce (see page 82); half a ball of buffalo mozzarella, chopped; some cherry tomatoes, cut in half; fennel stalks and basil leaves.

Cover the base with tomato sauce (see page 82), and top with anchovy fillets and rocket leaves.

Brush the base with olive oil. Arrange on it marinated artichoke hearts, cut in half, stoned olives and shavings of Parmesan. After baking, add chopped parsley or coriander and a squeeze of lemon.

Spread the base with pesto (see page 110), goats' cheese, thin slices of cooked red onion and pine nuts.

ROOTS AND SUNDAY LUNCH

As mellow yellow leaves tumble from the thinning trees, it is good to gather around the table for a late Sunday lunch, enjoying the last fiery orange nasturtiums displayed in a jug and lighting candles as dusk falls.

Butter, lemon and herb roasted chicken

serves 4–6

A flavoursome roast chicken should be lavished with plenty of herbs, lemon, butter and sea salt and stuffed with an onion. The onion's aromatic quality makes or breaks a roast chicken. Peel a whole one and stuff it in the chicken's cavity along with slices of lemon and thyme. Onions were highly prized during the war, when their growing was restricted in favour of less nutrient-greedy potatoes or cabbages. It was recorded that a single onion made £4 3s at a raffle (about £107.69 in today's prices) and the winner managed to eke out the flavour of the onion in her cooking for a whole month before actually eating it. Now that's what I call thrifty.

Even the skins have their use, according to the historian Dorothy Hartley, who wrote *Food in England*[14] in 1954: '*The papery golden skins of onions should not be thrown away. They are good natural colouring for soups and stews. Broth should always be made golden and delectable by cooking the skins in it.*'

handful of rosemary or thyme, roughly chopped
handful of parsley, roughly chopped
3 garlic cloves, roughly chopped
grated rind and juice of 1 lemon
125g/4oz/1 stick unsalted butter, softened
1 x 1.5kg/3lb free-range chicken

for the stuffing
1 onion
couple of sprigs of thyme or rosemary
½ lemon
sea salt and freshly ground black pepper

Mix the herbs, garlic and lemon rind and juice with the softened butter. Season with sea salt and freshly ground black pepper. Lift the skin by the chicken breast and push the herb butter in, smoothing it across the flesh. Stuff the bird's cavity with the onion, rosemary sprigs and lemon.

To get the breast meat really juicy and moist, it's a good idea to roast the chicken breast-side down until the last 15 minutes or so of cooking, when it can be turned upright to crisp the skin.

Place in an oven preheated to 180°C/350°F/Gas Mark 4, and cook for about an hour, depending on the size of the bird (allow 20 minutes per 500g/1lb). Baste several times during the cooking to keep the bird moist. I like to throw a few carrots and peeled shallot onions in during the last half an hour or so of cooking. The chicken is cooked if the juices run clear when a skewer is inserted right into the thickest part of the thigh. If there is any sign of pink, return the bird to the oven for a few minutes and test again.

Three easy things to do with chicken leftovers

Chicken with tarragon cream: really tasty and looks as if you've made much more effort than you have.

Heat a couple of tablespoons of olive oil in a pan and add a few chopped spring onions, a chopped garlic clove, a handful of chopped tarragon, and the grated rind and juice of half a lemon, and cook for a few minutes.

Add chopped pieces of cooked chicken (chuck out the skin and any fatty bits) and cook for a few more minutes. Add a small pot of double cream.

Stir and, when everything is thoroughly reheated, serve immediately with whatever you fancy – perhaps some potato slices roasted in the oven, and maybe a salad or a big bowl of peas with mint.

Chicken, leek and parsley pie (see page 232).

Chicken stock (see page 235), which can be frozen and used as a tasty base for soups and risottos.

Roasted veg
See over for picture

The rich yellows of pumpkins, squashes and carrots and the beetroot pinks add wonderful colour to a fall lunch.

Chop up your favourite root vegetables, and roast them in a tray for about 45 minutes in an oven preheated to 180°C/350°F/Gas Mark 4, with plenty of extra virgin olive oil, garlic (halved bulbs or in cloves), and sea salt and freshly ground black pepper.

A fall salad

There are still a few bitter and peppery rocket leaves in the vegetable patch, which can be tossed with a crunchy lettuce from the greengrocer.

Make a simple dressing with extra virgin olive oil, Dijon mustard, lemon juice, sea salt and freshly ground black pepper.

And for pudding...

Fall's harvest of plump sweet fruits dictate that pudding should be Plum tart (see page 181) or a rich Apple and ginger pudding (see page 173), or maybe a refreshing Blackberry sorbet (see page 179). Or if that's all too much, simply a plate of golden brown russet apples with a piece of hard Cheddar or Manchego cheese.

A VISUAL TONIC

Wading through layers of papery leaves is sensual, like eating a Bendicks Bittermint or lazing on hot sand. The park glitters in the still, clear air during my early morning dog walk, the light as intense as the sweet liquorice smell from the dried fennel sprig I pick and crush in my hand.

The fall of leaves is a breathtaking wonder of nature, almost making you forget that summer is over. So much colour. So many variations on yellow, burnt orange and brown. This visual tonic is more energizing than herbal Floradix, the liquid plant food for humans, which my friend Bea swears by when she needs perking up.

Printing with leaves

Why can't art be something that is unpretentious and as simple as leaves printed on paper (see page 160)? It's important to have the confidence to furnish your home with things that please you, not what is fashionable or bought for investment.

You can do this at any time of the year, although fall is more fun because of the range of leaves that literally fall at your feet. Dry leaves work as long as they are flat.

Print surfaces

Printing on fabric is also easy; natural textures such as cotton and linen are good.

Avoid printing on shiny paper, as paint doesn't stick well to it. Most other paper is fine.

leaves, green or dry
scrap paper and old newspapers
2.5–5cm (1–2 inch) flat brush
water-based acrylic paint or fabric paint
tweezers
paper or fabric to print on
paint roller

Cover the work surface with a layer of old newspaper. Choose a leaf and place it face down on clean scrap paper.

Brush the leaf underside with paint, remembering that the thinner the paint, the more defined the veins will be. Pick up the leaf with tweezers and place it paint-side down on the paper (or fabric). Hold the leaf in place with one hand and use the other hand to cover it with another piece of scrap paper.

Use the roller or your fingers to press the paint from the leaf onto the paper. Remove the scrap paper, and carefully lift up the leaf without smudging the paint.

Shapes to look out for on a fall walk

ovate

digitate

pinnate

cleft

truncate

THE FALL GARDEN

The last swim at the lido, golden and still, with maturing shadows; the air warm but with a chill; the water sparkling and fresh. A wistful mood, now that there won't be any more swimming until spring. But to look on the bright side, there are dahlias – English garden staples with flouncy petals that make me think of the hip fashion designer Erdem Moralioglu's digital floral-print dresses, one of which would be top of any flower lover's wish list.

Dahlias are another last blast of gorgeous fall colour before the dankness of winter begins. This native Mexican flower, which was imported 200 years ago, has always been a mainstay of the allotment garden, to pick for the table along with the cabbages and beans.

I remember my grandfather, a hardware-shop owner, fag in mouth, carefully tying his prize purple spiky blooms to stakes with green hairy string.

In more elevated gardening circles though, the frilly dahlia was long considered somewhat vulgar. I'm glad the style bibles and garden columns have made them acceptable again, both in and outside the vegetable patch. There are wonderful varieties for any border or pot. One of my favourites is Noreen, a flirty, rich pink pompom shape.

The fall vegetable patch

The last shallots and potatoes have been lifted, bean seeds have been saved in paper bags for next spring, the garlic has been plaited and hung in the shed and the apples are wrapped up snugly in newspaper for eating through the winter. I plant out spring cabbages that have been sown in August and take the last tomatoes inside to pinken a little and to throw in a last fresh-from-the-garden tomato sauce.

In November I'll sow the hardiest varieties of broad beans, Aquadule Claudia, straight into the ground. The seeds should start to germinate within two or three weeks, although they may not appear above the ground until the new year. I cover the rows to prevent mice and birds from eating seeds and young plants; I use green mesh netting quite successfully. November sowings do better in colder winters rather than wet ones. If the seeds do germinate well, the crop is earlier and heavier because the plants develop good root systems in the cool conditions.

Rotating your vegetables

Think about rotating your vegetables so that the same ones aren't grown in the same patch of soil each year, thus reducing its fertility. An exception is onions, which can be grown in the same place year after year.

Putting the garden to bed

It is satisfying to trim, sweep and neaten up the withered remnants of summer's wild growth.

I snip the lavenders so that they are more rounded and bushy, but I don't go mad trying to make them look topiary perfect. I should have collected the dried flower heads in summer, when they were at their most pungent, but there are enough aromatic handfuls to rescue from the flower stalks to make lavender bags for Christmas presents. A whiff of lavender is almost as good as ginger and lemon tea for getting me off to sleep.

Making a lavender bag

Cut off the stalks and dry the heads of lavender on sheets of newspaper.

Make an inner bag to hold the heads by cutting two pieces of cotton, putting their right sides together, stitching on three sides, then turning the pocket right side out. Stuff this with the heads, then turn under the open edges and stitch. Place inside the outer bag – which can be made from whatever you like. A muslin envelope is lovely, or you can make simple bags from fabric remnants tied at the neck with ribbon. I squash them in drawers for fragrant knickers or hang them among my best clothes to help repel a moth attack.

Planting bulbs for spring colour

Isn't online shopping wonderful? Waking up to the doorbell and a postman bearing a cardboard box with perforated holes and my order: *Tulipa* Lilac Perfection, White Parrot and Violet Beauty. Gorgeous colour for next spring.

The most important thing about bulbs is to make sure you plant them the right way up: the hairy root bit at the bottom and the pointy shoot at the top. If in doubt, plant them sideways, as the shoot will find its way to the light. Plant them 15cm (6 inches) deep to keep out the foxes and squirrels, who enjoy a crunchy bulb or two … or three … or more. By the way, many ybulbs are poisonous if eaten by humans and can be irritating to the skin.

My favourite bulbs:

Crocus: splashes of optimistic white and green among the winter greyness.

Tulip: White Parrot with frilly petals.

Allium christopii: huge purple, starry globe flowers.

Narcissi: sweetly scented 'Tete-a-Tete'.

Grape hyacinth: mainly blue, some white.

Hyacinth: white and blue.

Bluebell: scented and pretty, especially the dwarf scillas.

Forcing bulbs for indoor winter scent

If there's anything that you should buy ASAP in early fall, it is a good supply of bulbs specially prepared for forcing. They soon run out at the local garden centre. White narcissi, hyacinths and crocuses are top sellers, and it's most irritating to be left with a paltry choice of yellow crocuses or yellow crocuses! To ensure blooms for Christmas, plant them during the second week of November.

Ideally use a pot with a drainage hole, but I find that with careful watering it's perfectly possible to use a container without one. This means you can have much more fun and pot up in your favourite bowls and basins, such as the blue and white enamel bowls that I use (see opposite).

Place a small amount of compost in the bottom of the pot. Plant the bulbs with the tips pointing upwards. Leave at least 2.5cm (1 inch) between bulbs. Fill the pot with compost until the bulbs are just covered, or with the tips just showing. Place the bowl in a cool dark place. Too much light and too warm a temperature will cause the shoots to develop faster than the roots.

Water weekly, making sure you water the compost and not the top of the bulb. Keep moist but do not over-water.

When the shoots are about 10cm (4 inches) tall and fully green, move the container to a sunny but cool spot, avoiding direct sun. The shoots will continue to grow and in about two to three weeks you will have flowers.

The flowers will last longer in a cool spot out of direct sunlight. Turn the pot occasionally, as the flowers will grow towards the light.

More fall planting: wallflowers and roses

Wallflowers arrive at garden centres in early fall in unprepossessing bundles of green stems with muddy roots. These wonderfully old-fashioned English flowers can be grown in borders, pots and window boxes. Their flowers come in shades of yellow, white, pink and orange, like faded floral prints on pieces of old chintz, and in single colours. Creamy white's a favourite too.

I can't think of a more lovely start to a late spring day than standing on the steps outside the kitchen with a coffee, warm coat over pyjamas, and the wallflowers' heady marzipan scent.

Wallflowers will grow in most soils as long as they are free-draining. Don't plant them too late – frosts and icy weather will kill their roots. They need a sunny position, preferably sheltered from the wind.

A rose for winter

(see page 144 for rose varieties)

Prepare roses for planting in November. When planting roses in the ground, ideally double dig, which means two spits deep – that is about 25–30cm (10–12 inches). On heavy soils put some gravel, pebbles or sand in the lower spit, together with manure, seaweed and straw. For the top spit use compost, leaf mould, plus a large handful of bonemeal.

You can also grow roses in pots. Imagine gorgeous old English pink blooms on even the most urban balconies or terrace. They must have space, though, so use a large container of at least 40cm diameter by 28cm depth (16 x 11 inches) to give the roots more room to develop and to help prevent the soil from drying out too quickly. They must be fed and watered regularly throughout the summer.

Grow your own fruit for apple pie

Start planting fruit trees. You don't need masses of space. See opposite for some ideas. As one of my blog readers, who has a passion for quinces, says, *'Quince trees are very easy to grow – small and elegant. I have planted one in the small town garden of every house I've lived in. The fruit looks beautiful hanging on the trees, and its scent is exquisite in a room. I would never be without one.'*

When preparing the soil for fruit trees, you must dig deep and make sure it is well drained. Fruit trees can't flourish through the winter if their roots are waterlogged. Work manure into the hole and take out stones.

Dig a wide hole so you can spread the roots out well, and if the tree needs a stake, put that in first and arrange the roots around it. Soak dry tree roots before planting. If you're not ready to plant, don't leave them tied up in a bundle or with their roots exposed. Dig a trench in a corner somewhere, and get the roots covered with soil as quickly as possible. They will be safe until you are ready to plant them properly.

Trees in pots
For balconies and pot gardens, plant compact fruit trees in tubs with broad bases.

Looking after the apple tree

This year we had a light crop of apples, probably because I didn't thin out the very heavy crop of fruit last summer, which means it had very little energy to develop fruit buds. After the last apples have turned to a fruity mush on the grass, I give the tree a 'haircut' – a good tidy up with the loppers, taking out all the dead wood, and trimming the wayward shoots. A gardening friend of mine says that in summer, when the trees are in full growth, you ought to be able to throw an apple through the tree without touching a twig!

Shapes for fruit trees

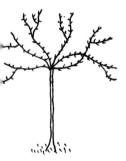  

standard
A tall tree, with a main stem about 2m (6 or 7ft) high. Good for a suburban back garden.

cordon
Good for the small garden – a single stem, without branches.

bush
A spreading tree on a short stem – needs more space.

espalier
Branches are trained horizontally. Good for fences, by a path or the back of a border.

Good things to eat in winter: swede, turnips, curly kale, Seville oranges, carrots, red cabbage, cabbage, chicory, forced rhubarb, dried figs, dates, broad beans, pomegranates, lemons.

winter

I like to walk the dog in the muffled silence that follows an overnight coating of snow. She skitters and slides for sticks while I tuck my hands deeper into my pockets and think about how to make a thick, warming vegetable soup for lunch. Winter isn't all deep, dark, short-day gloom. It's breathtaking when frost shatters on the shed windowpanes and the garden looks like a delicate and perfect iced winter vision. Then there are fires with beguiling flames that seem to insist we leave desktop screens to engage with the heat, and peel an aromatic clementine or two. Winter is an excuse to wrap up and be snug; to spend more than I should on white Victorian crocheted blankets. My justification is that it's better to be warm with natural textures than to crank up the heating. Winter is the season to disappear into the kitchen and the comforting fug and aroma of making marmalade.

PORRIDGE AND BLANKETS

Snow! '–5°C and we're all going snowwhere' shout the headlines as a white Narnia descends upon London and suspends the daily grind. Our ordinary street is now a heavenly avenue with snow-laden branches bejewelling the view. The sound that snow makes as it packs under your boots! The velvety swish of car tyres on untreated streets. Instead of fussing about interest rates and deadlines, we find ourselves asking 'how do you roll a snowman?', 'what have you done with the sledge?', æcan I build an igloo in the garden?'

At the park I hear whoops and cheers, as if it is a blazing summer's day at the beach. Monday has been cancelled, along with school and all of London's buses. The entire city surrenders to delight. It's a scene one barely witnesses in London, one of innocence: snow in a city that doesn't do extremes of weather.

Thus, unused to these conditions, one of the teenagers is nursing her first crop of itchy chilblains, hastened by her lack of enthusiasm for sensible (uncool) walking boots. I explain – the 'without judgement' style of explaining – that flimsy pumps are probably not the best option for negotiating slush, grit and skating-rink pavements.

Bowls of hot porridge

Even if the footwear advice is not welcomed, at least the suggestion that everyone keeps warm with bowls of hot porridge at breakfast is met with approval; they are not only comforting, they are ideal vehicles for large amounts of dark muscovado sugar or golden syrup.

I make it (enough for 3–4 people) with roughly 1 cup of jumbo rolled oats to 3 cups of water. Bring the ingredients to the boil in a saucepan and simmer gently for 5–10 minutes, until creamy. Add more water if necessary, and stir regularly to stop it sticking. Honey, butter, cream, crème fraîche or chopped dates are other delights to eat with porridge.

Muscovado sugar

Muscovado sugar, from *mascabado* (meaning unrefined), also known as 'Barbados sugar' or 'poor man's sugar', is unrefined, natural cane sugar. Much better for you than refined sugar, it has all of the natural ingredients of sugar cane but with a delicious rich toffee taste. When I ran out of caster, I substituted it with muscovado in the sponge recipe on page 151 and it makes the sponge beautifully rich in taste and colour, even if it is a little heavier.

Of course, some people don't do sweet things in their porridge, and just add salt (my mother was a butter and salt person). Each to their own.

Remember to avoid 'porridge pan' (it's the same with scrambled eggs) by soaking the remains in water immediately. That way you wont have to waste time with a scourer, which is not good for most pans.

Oatmeal is a meal, like a coarse flour. It comes in varying degrees of coarseness, ranging from the roughest (usually referred to as 'pinhead' oatmeal), which is an oat grain cut into about 8 pieces, to completely smooth. I use a medium meal for oat biscuits (see page 225). My friend Sarah makes her porridge with medium oatmeal, soaking it in double the volume of cold water overnight, then the next morning slowly bringing it to the boil, whisking regularly and adding more water until it's neither too stiff nor too soft.

Rolled oats are grains of oats that have been rolled flat until they are papery. This means that they are fairly powdery and so will absorb liquid quickly, which is why you only have to cook them for 2-3 minutes to get porridge.

Jumbo oats are not rolled as heavily and are coarser. I love them not only in porridge, but also for flapjacks (see page 190).

Elevenses and homework

In theory, eating a good slow-release complex carbohydrate such as porridge oats at breakfast-time will keep hunger pangs at bay. In practice, however, writing this book, filling in ridiculous forms, making difficult phone calls, all lead me long before lunch to the biscuit tin to find something sweet, unhealthy and comforting (yes, we do bad food, too). Fat chance. Someone else will have got there first. I try to keep healthy snacks in the desk drawer for nibbling on – dried figs, apricots or some juicy raisins.

Oat biscuits

makes 20

Homemade oat biscuits are useful weapons against rolls of fat from biscuit tin displacement activity.

275g/9oz/3 cups medium oatmeal
¼ tsp baking soda
pinch of sea salt
1½ tbsp unsalted butter, melted
about 175ml/6fl oz/¾ cup water

Place the oatmeal, baking soda and sea salt in a bowl. Make a well in the centre, add the melted butter and stir in with a wooden spoon, together with enough of the water to make a stiff paste.

Knead for a few minutes. Put on a floured board and roll out as thinly as possible. Cut into circles or triangles, transfer to a greased baking sheet and place in an oven preheated to 200°C/400°F/Gas Mark 6, for 20–30 minutes.

Cool on a wire rack. Eat plain or with butter and jam. Store in an airtight tin for freshness, but heat them up if you like your oat biscuits warm.

A calm work space

Working from home is, on the whole, a pleasant experience, with no sweaty commuting or office dragons. But as domestic intrusions are inevitable – the dog snaffling a cake from my photo shoot set-up, warring teenagers, a very sweet old lady (a Jehovah's Witness in disguise) at the door, and so on – it is essential to make one's work space as calm and ordered as possible.

My key elements include a decent-sized desk – mine is an old oak school desk from a junk shop, painted white. I am not keen on impersonal, corporate-style laminated shapes. It feels more pleasurable to work at a surface that is pleasing to touch and look at as well as being functional.

My work chair is one of my Ercol dining chairs, comfortable and supportive when a cushion is wedged between back and chair. I invested in floor-to-ceiling shelves in two alcoves, where I store my reference books, magazines and work-files in flat-pack boxes made of white card. For close study work there is a simple flexible anglepoise light, and inspiration comes from a great big pinboard made from stick-on cork tiles, washed in a pale blue emulsion and plastered with photos, cards and colours that get me thinking (see page 153).

FROSTS AND HOT PIES

This is the season for shutting doors and hoping that the boiler does not break down. Reading in bed at night, swathed in an array of colourful wraps and blankets to keep warm, I'm told I look like an eccentric aunt. How romantic! One of my favourite blankets is a cotton cellular one that I dyed lilac to pep up its hospital look.

All my blankets are brought out and draped and layered over beds and sofas. Good to curl up with in front of a film.

Draught exclusion becomes an obsession in our Victorian house with its rattly sash windows. I am running up a couple of sausage-shaped draught excluders in blue-and-white striped ticking. Filled with old newspaper they're great for stuffing against the howling gales that blow under the back doors. I am also thinking about a double-lined blanket curtain to hang on a rod on the inside of the front door at night.

Emergency rations and other forms of resourceful cooking

In the manner of diluting white emulsion paint to make it go further, or patching and darning sheets, I enjoy making things stretch. If this all sounds a bit worthy and parsimonious, it's not meant to. I like to think of it as, well, more of a creative challenge.

The other day, for example, there was a family meltdown over a car that had broken down. Not expecting to have to dish anything up that evening, but now landed with a driver and passengers going nowhere, I knew stomachs should be filled in order to ameliorate the general bad mood, and let me get back to my Henning Mankell thriller. I poked around in the fridge, and was very excited to find some cold beef from Sunday's lunch – someone had usefully hidden it under a plate

A quick supper with frozen peas

There are usually several bags of frozen peas in the freezer – well, petit pois to be precise, because these are the sweetest of peas, and really do taste like the ads say. You can get away with making the most wonderful instant supper by adding pieces of fried bacon and a few mint sprigs to a bowl of steaming peas (I always cook them from frozen and just until they're hot through – a few minutes). Frozen peas make a good ice pack for bruises too.

of apple crumble remains. I cut the beef into thin sticks and fried it in a little sesame oil with a few spring onions and some garlic. With shakings of soy sauce over some fluffy and steaming Thai rice from the bulk-buy sack in the larder, this shining example of leftovers-to-the-rescue (the culinary equivalent of iron-on hem tape) restored stomachs and family peace.

And then there's the whole anti-food-waste issue to consider. I was brought up with the concept of not wasting food because both my parents were World War II children, and endured rationing.

My daughter, though, sees little harm in binning a perfectly good but one day out-of-date yogurt: 'Mum, you'll give us all food poisoning,' she protests. It would be good to line up a date with Tristram Stuart, whose book *Waste: Uncovering the Global Food Scandal* reveals how much food gets chucked away right across the food supply system.

Consider this: from the bread and other grain-based products that British households throw away each year, Stuart estimates that it would be possible to alleviate the hunger of 30 million people. That sounds at first like an improbably large number, until one considers that British households chuck away 2.6 billion slices of bread each year.

Cheese on toast

Simply grill bread on one side, spread the non-toasted side with butter and Dijon mustard, top with thin slivers of cheese and grill until bubbling.

Customize your cheese on toast with leftovers or a store cupboard rummage: a few slices of tired ham, the ends of cheese, an egg, they are all worthy.

What's often a solitary treat can be adapted to something more substantial and good-looking if you serve it with a few dressed salad leaves.

Potato and fish cakes

serves 4 (2 cakes each)

This is a really good way of calling upon your stocks of canned fish when you don't know what to do for a quick supper/lunch.

400g/13oz mashed potato (see the recipe on page 195)
200g/7oz tinned wild salmon
4 spring onions, finely chopped
salt and freshly ground black pepper

Combine all the ingredients to make round cake shapes. Dip in flour and fry in butter on one side until crisp, then turn over and do the same on the other side.

For a simple sauce, mix chopped coriander and lemon juice into crème fraîche.

Shepherd's pie

serves 6

My shepherd's pie is made with leftover mash and what remains of a lamb shoulder minced in one of those old-fashioned metal grinders that clamp to the table. It's satisfying to feed tatty bits of meat into the hopper and, as you turn the long handle, watch the lengths of meat spaghetti emerge, ready for a new lease of life.

This is quite a tomatoey version of shepherd's pie, but if you're not a tomato fan you can substitute the can of tomatoes with more traditional meat stock and a shake or two of Worcestershire sauce. Using beef instead of lamb turns the recipe into a cottage pie.

1 tbsp extra virgin olive oil
1 onion, chopped
400g/13oz can tomatoes
1 tbsp tomato paste
500g/1lb minced cooked lamb
pinch of fresh thyme leaves
sea salt and freshly ground pepper
1kg/2lb mashed potato (see recipe on page 195)
Parmesan cheese (optional)

Heat the oil in a pan, add the onion and cook until soft. Add the tomatoes and tomato paste and cook for 10 minutes or so. Stir in the minced lamb and heat right through (if you use fresh mince, cook it for about 20 minutes). Add the thyme and seasoning and put into a pie dish. Top with the mashed potato, and draw a fork through to make furrows; these help make crispy bits on top.

Sometimes I grate Parmesan on the top. Although this isn't classic shepherd's pie material, it does taste delicious. Place in an oven preheated to 200°C/400°F/Gas Mark 6, for 30 minutes, until bubbling.

Chicken, leek and parsley pie

serves 4-6

see previous page

Good for when there's chicken left on the carcass of the roast, and you need to eat something with a comforting pastry crust.

for the filling

2 tbsp extra virgin olive oil
4 leeks, roughly chopped
2 garlic cloves, roughly chopped
400g/13oz cooked chicken, chopped
grated rind of 1 lemon
150ml/¼ pint/⅔ cup double cream
generous handful of parsley, roughly chopped
salt and freshly ground black pepper

for the pastry topping

200g/7oz rich shortcrust pastry (see recipe on page 181, omitting the sugar)
  or use ready-made shortcrust pastry
1 egg, beaten

For the filling, heat the oil in a pan and cook the leeks and garlic on a medium heat for 15 minutes or so. Stir in the chopped chicken, grated lemon rind, cream and parsley. Add salt and freshly ground black pepper. Put the mixture in a 1.5 litre/ 2½ pint/6 cup pie dish or tin.

Roll out the pastry on a floured surface and cut a 2.5cm (1 inch) wide strip, long enough to fit around the sides of the pie dish. Brush the rim of the pie dish with water and place the strip along it. This will hold the pastry cover in place.

Cut out the remaining pastry to 2.5cm/1 inch larger than the dish. Put a pie funnel in the middle of the dish to support the pastry. This stops it sinking and becoming soggy.

Place the pastry lid over the top and press the edges down to seal. Trim the excess pastry and crimp the sides with a fork.

Roll out the pastry trimmings, cut out shapes – leaves, hearts, diamonds, or whatever you conjure up – and arrange them on the surface. Brush the top with beaten egg and place in an oven preheated to 190°C/375°F/Gas Mark 5, for 30–35 minutes, until golden.

Bubble and squeak

serves 4-6

This is always a good thing to do with leftovers from Christmas lunch, and useful any time you've over-catered on the greens and potatoes.

250g/8oz leftover cooked cabbage or Brussels sprouts, or a mix of both
250g/8oz mashed potato
3 tbsp olive oil
freshly ground black pepper, and salt if you think it needs it

Chop the greens and mix with the mash in a bowl. Heat the oil in a frying pan and add the mixture, pressing it into the pan so that it is flat and even and covers the whole surface. Cook on a medium heat on both sides until it is crispy and hot all the way through.

Slow cooking

Holed up with hours of darkness ahead, flurries of snow beating at the window and the garden in a luminous blanket of white, the kitchen is the place to be. Lingering by the oven door with my laptop, I check that the meat and vegetable stew is coming on nicely.

A health and safety point: if you want to reheat the leftovers of a good stew, boil them thoroughly. As an impressionable eight-year-old, I took on board my father's story of visiting a patient with a violent stomach upset. He peeked in her larder and found a bubbling pot of meat stew – bubbling with bugs, that is, because she'd been gently warming it up each night, encouraging the microbes to multiply fantastically.

**A golden
winter stew**

serves 4–6

see page 234

This is a simple and nourishing kitchen staple for the winter and goes a long way if you stretch it with mashed potatoes, rice or couscous. (All students should include a stew in their repertoire.)

It might seem odd to use beer, but it adds a really rich flavour; the brand doesn't matter, but I think Guinness is particularly flavoursome. Brown meat is not the most inspiring of foods to look at, and so I like to use root vegetables such as carrots and swede for their golden colour, which goes so well with the green of the parsley or coriander. A long cooking time of 3 hours or so ensures tender meat and a rich, tasty gravy.

Adapt this basic stew recipe with:

A mixed bag of whatever's left in the veg basket – onion, turnip, tomato, cauliflower; a mixture of stock and red wine instead of beer; lamb or pork instead of beef. Stir in a couple of tablespoons of Thai green curry paste, or go in the Indian direction and mix in some ready-prepared garam masala paste and serve with rice.

3 tbsp plain flour
500g/1lb beef stewing steak, cut into small pieces and any fat removed
2 tbsp olive oil
250g/8oz swede, peeled and cut into thick sticks
250g/8oz carrots, peeled and cut into thick sticks
350ml/12fl oz/1½ cups beer, stock or wine
1 tbsp chopped fresh thyme
1 bay leaf
salt and freshly ground black pepper
1 tbsp chopped parsley, to garnish

Put the flour in a tough plastic bag, add the meat and shake until well coated. Heat the oil in a heavy based casserole and fry the meat, stirring for a few minutes, until brown. Add the vegetables and fry, continuing to stire for a few minutes longer. Add any remaining flour from the bag and stir in the beer, thyme, bay leaf and seasoning to taste.

Place in an oven preheated to 150°C/300°F/Gas Mark 2, with the lid on, and cook for 3 hours. I take it out a couple of times for a quick stir, and to check it's not drying out. If so, add more beer, stock or wine.

Scatter with chopped parsley. Delicious with various forms of potato, especially mash, gratin or baked spuds.

Stock up

You don't have to make your own stock every time; there are some really good concentrated ones. But that's not to say all stocks or concentrates are created equal. Our favourite stocks at home are Kallo organic chicken bouillon and Marigold vegetable stock.

But it really isn't much of a bother to throw a cooked chicken carcass or that of the leftover Christmas bird (turkey or pheasant) into a pan with onion, carrots, bay leaves, peppercorns and parsley. Fill it with water and leave to simmer for 2 or 3 hours. A lovely luxuriating way to fill the kitchen with warm and good homely smells on a frosty day.

Vegetable stock

Take your pick from the vegetable basket, and use up less than perky tops of leeks, mushroom stalks, outside leaves of cabbage, whatever is available.

Chop finely and put in a pan with boiling water, not quite covering, and add a bay leaf and some chopped thyme, marjoram and oregano (or pinches of dried herbs if you don't have access to fresh ones). Season with salt and freshly ground black pepper. Simmer for about half an hour, strain and use.

Fish stock

Make a tasty fish stock from shrimp and crab shells and the head and bones from a salmon, or ask for fish trimmings from the market or fishmonger.

Cover the fish pieces with cold water, and for every 500g/1lb of trimmings add an onion, a bay leaf, a small sprig of parsley and a teaspoon of lemon rind. Cover and boil for half an hour. Strain and use as a base for fish soup (see page 107).

NB: Cool, strain and keep all stocks in the fridge. Use within a day or two, or pour into plastic ice cube trays or bag and freeze.

A quick fish stew

For a fishy idea that evokes summer lunches by the seaside, add a few tablespoons each of fish stock and single cream to a pan with chunks of fish such as salmon or haddock fillet, that have been cooked lightly in a little butter and garlic. Cook the mixture for a few more minutes on a low heat until the fish is cooked through, and decorate with grated lemon zest and chopped parsley. Delicious with rice or pasta and a crisp green salad.

THE SIMPLE KITCHEN

If we're trying to save the planet I think it's good to downsize aspirations in the kitchen department. We need to reconsider our energy-hungry giant fridges belching crushed ice on tap and water-guzzling dishwashers.

I really don't think that everything has to be fitted wall to wall either. Apart from costing an arm and a leg in materials and construction, this can look so monotonous. Having said this, I think the classic fitted galley kitchen is brilliant for a really small space.

It can be great fun to trawl the junk shops for old storage cupboards and dressers that can be tarted up with a lick of paint; pieces that can go with you when you move.

My solution for storage is a long open shelf for plates, bowls, glasses and cups. It's good to be able to see what is what. Beneath this hangs a stainless steel pole with hooks for implements in constant use: colander, slotted spoons, ladle and so on.

The work surface is a tough wooden block board, which I sand to remove pot rings and oil with linseed oil once every three months or so. Other kit is kept in three drawers next to the cooker, including cutlery and things such as the whisk and corkscrew.

Three industrial-style glass pendant shades give good light. I can't stand those recessed downlighters; people often make the mistake of fitting too many.

Kitchen colour

Fresh, clean, no frills: white is a great kitchen colour. Over the years I have stirred, baked and idled by the radio in three white kitchens. The first was high up and part of an open-plan loft-style space. We revamped ugly blue kitchen units with white painted tongue-and-groove detailing. At the house in Spain, cooling breezes blew through the open doors and herb-scented air filled another bright white kitchen with cool terracotta flooring. And the glorious light-reflecting qualities of white persuaded me once again to decorate my current kitchen space with a white ceramic tile splashback and painted walls. I resisted white floors, knowing that we are all messy cooks prone to spilling indelible substances such as red wine or food colouring.

Those who claim that white is very emergency-room-like have a point, and indeed on really dreary days white can be quite cold, but only in the same way that any other colour loses its energy when daylight is not at its brightest. Any danger of the clinical can be avoided with tactile natural elements, such as wooden chairs, throws, simple china, and food itself; a simple bowl of green apples zings against white. Another way to offset any white starkness is to contrast woodwork, or features such as a dresser or shelving, in soft sludgy shades of grey or green. And just as in the rest of the house, I use warming splashes of colour in striped linen tea towels, retro aprons and a jug of greenery or flowers.

Kitchen kit

I like to have familiar things around me – my mum's old paring knife, the saggy metal cake rack, and the polka-dot pinny that I made up for my sewing book. I don't believe you have to spend a lot of money on sexy all-singing, all-dancing machines. I warm to the story that, after watching a *Masterchef* contestant use a food processor to chop nuts, designer Terence Conran pointed out to her that *'once you'd set up the machine, used it, disassembled it, cleaned it, and put it away again, it would have taken infinitely less time and effort to use a sharp knife'* (from *Design and Quality of Life* by Terence Conran[15]. His view, that in the end doing things the long way round may be much more effective, is typically sensible, and besides, so much of the enjoyment of cooking comes with using simple hands-on tools.

The first things I grab for stirring soups and stews are the worn, wooden spoons stuffed in a flowerpot on the kitchen counter. They have been accumulated on trips abroad and tracked down in back-street hardware stores.

My kitchen wouldn't be complete without pudding basins; basic and functional cream stoneware or white and blue-trimmed enamelware. Most people can remember licking their mum's cake mixture out of one of these. They come in different sizes. I use little ones to plant hyacinths in.

I make my first coffee of the morning in the small screw-top metal coffee pot, which burbles comfortingly when the coffee is ready.

I use heavy based saucepans with solid bottoms that will not buckle or burn the supper. Resist cheap and lightweight stuff; after a few months the handles will have worked loose and they'll be on the list of things to take to the dump.

My old friends are several very adult, almost pensionable cast-iron enamelled casseroles, which still work equally well when making soups and cooking vegetables on the hob as they do in the oven, nurturing something rich and nourishing (see A golden winter stew, in one of my favourite pans, on page 234).

The teenagers are into endless fry-ups, so I have splashed out on a stainless steel frying pan. It is bearing up well. Boiling water, a little detergent and a sponge deal with the worst burnt remains.

When the hordes descend, I use a giant two-handled stainless steel pan that will hold turkey and mushroom risotto for 15. It is also solid and safe when steaming sponge puddings and making jam and marmalade.

A heavy cast-iron ridged grill slab to put on the hob for vegetables, fish and meat creates that lovely charcoal-striped effect.

Flimsy knives are not only useless, but also perilous, and will lead you straight to Accident and Emergency at the local hospital. Like the pans, buy the best you can afford. Stainless steel is my choice. There are three sizes I use most: a small paring knife for chopping vegetables and herbs; a 15cm (6 inch) blade for tackling larger tasks, such as a pile of chopped onions; and a longer, 20cm (8 inch) number, which does for carving roasts and birds.

A simple metal colander for draining the lettuce is so much more tactile than the plastic revolving whizzers that manically suck the leaves dry, as is the method of wrapping them in a clean linen tea towel and giving them a good pat.

I use a hand-held kitchen whizzer to pulverize everything from soups to hummus. This, and a simple mixer with detachable paddles for whisking egg whites and cake mixture, is about the sum of my electronic gadgetry.

A WINTER PICK-ME-UP

One of my favourite remedies for chasing away winter gloom is to head off to whatever's showing in town and soak up the visual richness of Van Gogh's fizzing almond blossoms, say, or a Rothko colour-drenched canvas. I am inspired, refreshed and full of plans – if not to get out my dusty paintbrushes, at least to make myself a crisp winter salad of painterly colour, a still life for lunch.

Winter salad

Carrots and cabbage will do, nothing fancy or too exotic (we neglect what is grown in our own backyard). We need as much as we can get of raw, vitamin C concentrated goodness at this time of year. Give the dressing a kick by using lemon juice, or better still sour Seville orange juice (see more dressings on page 98)

2 or 3 carrots, peeled and sliced into thin sticks
200g/7oz/2 cups red cabbage, finely sliced
1 head of chicory, finely sliced
handful of pomegranate seeds
handful of chopped mixed nuts
few mint leaves, to garnish (my local Turkish shop has a steady supply all
   through the year)

for the dressing
1 tbsp extra virgin olive oil
2 tbsp Seville orange juice or lemon juice
1 garlic clove, finely chopped
salt and freshly ground black pepper

Combine the vegetables, pomegranate seeds and nuts in a bowl. In another small bowl, whisk the olive oil and orange or lemon juice until amalgamated. Add the garlic and season. Add the dressing to the salad, mix and garnish with mint.

WINTER WHITES

I've written about the delights of white more than enough in all my books, but it remains my touchstone for creating simple, light and space-enhancing interiors. And by the way, I know there are paint cards with 50 shades of white to boggle the eyes, but when you go to your local paint shop there is absolutely nothing wrong with asking for their best brilliant white matt emulsion.

White is timeless and the perfect blank canvas. A natural progression, then, for arts and crafts artists and architects, such as Voysey, Mackintosh and Morris, who championed the white interior as a reaction to the cluttered sombre look of the late 19th century.

More recently, architect John Pawson made a name for himself in the 1990s with his minimalist white spaces. He was part of a wider gang who weren't into the fussy chintz and prints of the 1980s fashion for English country house decoration.

White, like everything, has its limitations, and if you go for shiny surfaces and insist on everything being perfect, not a muddy pawprint in sight, then your home will look and feel sterile, like an operating theatre. But if you mix it with natural textures, matt finishes and battered-about-the-edges furniture it can look very friendly.

Cool, white and frosty

Even in the depths of dreary dull winter I aim to make my white-themed home feel airy and bright. I think it works, all this whiteness, because I try to contrast it with splashes of bright colour provided by my favourite rugs and throws. Nature is welcomed inside, too, to make the space more tactile, more alive. There are scented bulbs in pots (see page 217 on how to pot up), sprigs of rosemary on the mantelpiece,

a bowl of oranges or clementines and, at Christmas, the herby scented needles of a Christmas tree.

I am a homespun girl, and love making festive biscuits to hang on pieces of string, and other decorations such as wool and tissue pompoms. Although I yearn for southern light and warmth at this time of year, it's cheering to be snug at home with a blazing fire, flickering candles and the rich citrus aroma of orange peel.

Lemon meringue pie

serves 6

(see page 242)

Beat the winter blues with a cool, white, stylish pudding. A bit of a performance to make, but it's worth it to eat the mouth-watering combination of pastry, zingy lemon curd and fluffy meringue.

for the pastry
see rich sweet pastry recipe on page 181

for the lemon curd
grated rind and juice of 2 lemons
2 egg yolks
50g/2oz/½ stick butter
175g/6oz/generous ¾ cup sugar

for the meringue
2 egg whites
100g/3½oz/½ cup caster sugar

Prepare the pastry as for the Plum tart on page 181. Roll out and line a greased 23cm (9 inch) pie plate or flan ring and place it on a baking sheet. Prick the base of the pastry all over. Line with foil, weigh down with dried beans and bake in an oven preheated to 190°C/375°F/Gas Mark 5, for about 15 minutes. Remove the foil and return to the oven for 15 minutes, or until golden and crisp. Remove the flan ring, if you've used one, and cool. Reduce the heat to 180°C/350°F/Gas Mark 4.

To make the lemon curd: Place all the ingredients in a heatproof bowl over a pan of simmering water. Don't let the base of the bowl touch the simmering water. Stir until the sugar has dissolved and continue heating gently without boiling for about 20 minutes, or until the curd is thick enough to coat the back of a wooden spoon. When cool, layer the curd onto the tart base.

To make the meringue: Whisk the egg whites in a clean, dry, cool bowl until they stand in stiff peaks. Whisk in half the sugar, and then carefully fold in the remainder using a metal spoon. Pile the meringue on top of the pie to completely cover the lemon filling and bake for about 15–20 minutes until lightly browned.

A SIMPLE MODERN CHRISTMAS

Christmas is for swooping on slivers of sweet *jamón ibérico*, wild smoked salmon sent from a generous great aunt, or chocolate-covered figs that come in bright-coloured paper from Italy.

I am not interested in the endless countdowns to the perfect Christmas lunch. I want the occasion to be relaxed and delicious. It's hard enough keeping the family harmonious, without thinking that you've got to dish up a gourmet spread.

We like to ring the changes, from roast piglet (awkward to fit in the oven) in Spain one year and a large salmon baked in foil another, to rib of beef or a turkey with all the trimmings. There are also classic family favourites, such as Mushroom and chestnut stuffing for birds (see page 167) and a rich Christmas pudding stuffed with 50-pence pieces, which we set on fire, like pyromaniacs, in a pool of heated brandy.

Christmas pudding

This recipe makes two large puddings. Put one away, and let it mature for next year – or crack it open when you want to.

The last Sunday before the first Sunday in Advent is Stir-up-Sunday, traditionally the day for making Christmas pud. However, I have thrown puddings together only a few days before Christmas, and they taste perfectly good.

This recipe is from my mum's plastic box file of recipes written on spattered card, torn out from magazines, or typed on thin paper by friends at the tennis club. The original recipe includes barley wine, but I shouldn't think anyone drinks it today. Beer is a perfectly good substitute.

for 2 x 1 litre/1¾ pint/4 cup pudding basins
225g/7¼oz/1¼ cups currants
225g/7¼oz/1¼ cups sultanas
350g/11½oz/2 cups raisins
175g/6oz/1 cup candied peel
110g/3¾oz/generous ½ cup almonds
225g/7½oz/1⅔ cups self-raising flour
225g/7½oz/4 cups fresh breadcrumbs

225g/7½oz/1¾ cups vegetarian suet
½ tsp sea salt
2 tbsp mixed spice
½ tsp grated nutmeg
350g/11¾oz/1½ cups demerara or muscovado sugar
grated rind and juice of 1 lemon
450g/14½oz/1½ cups orange marmalade
6 eggs, well beaten
250ml/8fl oz/1 cup beer
4 tbsp brandy or rum

Mix all the dry ingredients together. Add the lemon rind and juice, the marmalade and the beaten eggs. Mix in half the beer and stir well. Cover with a clean tea towel and leave for 24 hours. Add the rest of the beer and the brandy or rum. Beat well.

Turn into greased basins and cover with greaseproof paper tied with string and foil. Put into boiling water and steam in a pan over boiling water on the hob for 4 hours. Ensure the pudding does not touch the water. Steam for another 2–3 hours before eating the pudding.

Peppermint creams

Makes 24

You'd think that being a stylist and thus a quasi 'professional' shopper, I would be resistant to the frisson of panic induced by beguiling and glossy gift lists in the pre-Christmas press. I try not to look. I mix shop-bought things (secondhand glass is always good) with some homemade items. I can't see a teenager wowing over a box of peppermint creams but know that if they're prettily wrapped in tissue they will really please a girlfriend or grandparent.

1 egg white
450g/14½oz/4 cups icing sugar
2 tbsp lemon juice
5 or 6 drops of peppermint flavouring
the mere droplet of green colouring (or they'll look horrid)

Beat the egg white until fluffy, then add all the other ingredients to make a ball of green paste. Roll out to half an inch thick and cut out shapes. I like mine round, but stars and hearts would be good for Christmas too. Decorate with silver balls and leave the creams to dry on greaseproof paper overnight.

Quick Christmas biscuits

Christmas biscuits can be eaten for tea, wrapped up as a gift, or hung on the tree.

Use the shortbread recipe on page 66 to make the dough. I add a little water or milk before forming it into a ball – this helps to bind the ingredients and make rolling out easier. Roll out on a floured surface. Cut into shapes (hearts or stars), transfer to a greased baking sheet and place in an oven preheated to 190°C/375°F/Gas Mark 5, for 10–15 minutes. Leave to cool on a wire rack and then ice (mix 175g/6oz/1½ cups icing sugar with a little water) and decorate with silver balls.

Elderflower jellies

Makes 8

Try using 600ml/1 pint /2½ cups Spanish cava for another jelly idea.

For refreshing flavour with a summery flowery taste, I make jellies with last year's elderflower fizz (see page 19).

Soften 5 sheets of gelatine in a bowl with 3 tablespoons of cold water for 10 minutes then melt over a pan of simmering water. Add to a jug containing 450ml/¾ pint/scant 2 cups elderflower fizz and 150ml/¼ pint/generous ½ cup water. Stir the liquids and pour into glasses. Leave to set in the fridge for a few hours.

The sweet taste of oranges

Driving by neat, sunlit orange groves, inhaling the sweet heady blossomed air floating through the half-opened car window, was as much part of Christmas in Andalucia as stocking up with bulging nets of *navelinas* (the ones without pips) sold at the roadside. The matt texture of an unwaxed orange is so much more appealing than artificially shined ones sold in the supermarket.

At Christmas lunch and the festive meals that follow, we still enjoy the clean, fresh taste of sliced oranges. Carefully slice the peel off with a very sharp knife, cut the orange into wafer-thin discs, and chill in the refrigerator with a little lemon juice, a tablespoon or two of Cointreau and a few fresh mint leaves.

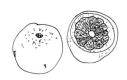

Orange and almond cake

Makes 1 x 20cm (8 inch) cake

This near-Eastern-inspired cake is an aromatic alternative to the obvious repertoire of Christmas desserts or teatime ideas. It is also flour-free, so good for anyone with a wheat allergy. The cake has a tendency to stick to the bottom of the tin, so make sure the tin is properly greased and floured – a loose-bottomed tin enables easier removal.

4 eggs, separated
grated rind of 2 oranges
100g/3½oz/¾ cup ground almonds
125g/4oz/⅔ cup caster sugar

for the syrup
juice of 4 oranges
125g/4oz/⅔ cup caster sugar

Mix together the egg yolks, orange rind, almonds and caster sugar. Beat the egg whites until stiff and fold into the yolk mixture. Pour into a greased and floured loose-bottomed 20cm (8 inch) round cake tin.

Place in an oven preheated to 180°C/350°F/Gas Mark 4, for about 45 minutes, or until a skewer plunged into the middle comes out clean. Leave to cool before removing from the tin.

To make the syrup: Put the orange juice and sugar in a small saucepan and bring to the boil. Simmer for about 15 minutes, until the liquid thickens. Leave to cool. Using a fork, spike the cake with holes and pour over the syrup.

How to make a rosemary wreath

A simple idea to decorate a shelf, mantelpiece or the Christmas table.

120cm/4ft of garden wire
a good handful of rosemary sprigs
string
scissors
ribbon

Finishing touches
A check ribbon bow,
a nice piece of velvet
ribbon or white linen
tape will also look good.

Bend the wire in half and twist the ends together to make a circle. Continue to wind the ends of the wire upon itself to secure. Weave the rosemary between the wire until the latter is covered. Tie the stems in place with lengths of string – I like hairy gardener's string the best because it looks natural.

I don't think it's always necessary to have a pudding, but it's always useful to have a bowl of walnuts to crack and eat with some thin slivers of *membrillo* and hard Spanish Manchego cheese. All delicious with a little glass of sweet muscatel wine.

Membrillo ice-cream
Quince paste ice-cream
Serves 4-6

(for homemade lemon ice-cream see page 133)

Another way we like to enjoy the flavour of quince is to make homemade *membrillo* ice-cream to serve with simple fork biscuits. Its appley fragrance transports me to Spain and the little orchard of quinces by a stream. The delicate white spring blossoms were replaced by furry golden orbs, which we'd pick in autumn and boil up to make the delicious paste.

100g/3½oz *membrillo*, homemade (see page 183) or ready-made
300ml/½ pint/1¼ cups double cream, whipped

Melt the *membrillo* in a pan on a medium heat in a couple of tablespoons of water. Cool and fold the melted paste into the cream. Freeze.

Serve with simple fork biscuits: Cut 110g/4oz/1 stick butter into pieces and rub into 150g/5oz/1 cup self-raising flour. Stir in 50g/2oz/¼ cup sugar and the grated rind of a lemon. Form into a sausage shape. Chill in the refrigerator for an hour, then cut into thin slices. Put on a greased baking sheet and run a fork over each one. Place in an oven preheated to 180°C/350°F/Gas Mark 4, for 10–15 minutes. Cool on a wire rack.

Easy mince pies
makes 12–18

I whack out large numbers of mince pies before, during and after the festivities and find it less hassle to use ready-made shortcrust pastry, plus some good ready-made mincemeat. I make it my 'own' with brandy, freshly grated lemon and orange rind and a handful of pine nuts, leaving the mixture to marinate for a few hours.

200g/7oz ready-made shortcrust pastry
1 egg, beaten
200g/7oz/generous 1 cup mincemeat
dusting of icing sugar

Roll out the pastry on a floured surface. Cut out circles with an 8cm (3¼ inch) pastry cutter and line a greased bun tin. Brush the rims with beaten egg. Fill with dollops of mincemeat. Cut out same-sized lids and fit on top. Brush with a little beaten egg and place in an oven preheated to 180°C/350°F/Gas Mark 4, for 15 minutes. Cool on a wire rack and dust with caster or sifted icing sugar.

THE JOY OF CHOCOLATE

I eat chocolate all year round, but it's most beguiling and comforting in the winter.

Chocolate pots
serves 4

A chocolate pot is like a little black dress – classic, simple and stylish.

175g/6oz chocolate (minimum 70% cocoa solids)
2 tbsp brandy
6 eggs
grated orange zest decoration

Melt the chocolate with the brandy in a bowl over a pan of simmering water. Stir until smooth. Remove from the heat.

Separate the eggs and add the yolks to the melted chocolate, beating in each one with a wooden spoon. Whip the whites until they stand in stiff peaks. Stir one-third into the chocolate mixture, then fold in the remaining white with a metal spoon.

Spoon into glass dishes and put in the fridge. Decorate with a little grated orange zest and serve.

Chestnut and chocolate truffles
makes about 36

These are little moreish jewels that could be put in a box lined with tissue paper to give to a friend, or eaten with little cups of coffee after a meal.

100g/3½oz/scant 1 stick unsalted butter, cut into small pieces
100g/3½oz/½ cup sugar
200g/7oz chocolate (minimum 70% cocoa solids), broken into pieces
200g/7oz/1⅓ cups cooked peeled chestnuts, chopped
3 egg yolks
200ml/7fl oz/scant 1 cup double cream
cocoa powder, to serve

Melt the butter, sugar and chocolate in a pan over a low heat. Mix thoroughly. Leave to cool for 30 minutes, then add the chestnuts, egg yolks and cream. Mix well, then refrigerate, covered, for a couple of hours until firmish.

Remove from the fridge. For each truffle, take 2 teaspoons of mixture and roll into a roughly shaped ball. Place on a foil-lined baking sheet and chill overnight. Roll in cocoa powder just before serving.

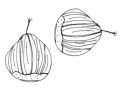

Chocolate and chestnut cake

makes about 10 slices

Serve cold from the refrigerator, cut into small squares for tea. It's also good for pudding with a little cream and sweet wine.

400g/13oz/2⅔ cups peeled chestnuts, chopped
125g/4oz/⅔ cup caster sugar
125g/4oz chocolate (minimum 70% cocoa solids), broken into chunks
100g/3½oz/scant 1 stick unsalted butter

for the icing
125g/4oz chocolate (minimum 70% cocoa solids)
1 tbsp butter
1 tbsp fresh orange juice
1 tbsp grated orange zest

Mix the chestnuts and sugar together until smooth; it's best to use a food processor. Melt the chocolate and butter in a large saucepan. Stir in the chestnut/sugar paste until smooth. Turn into a 20cm (8 inch) greased square cake tin.

To make the icing: Melt the chocolate with the butter, orange juice and zest, and stir until smooth. Pour over the chestnut and chocolate base, and chill in the fridge overnight.

HOW TO MAKE MARMALADE GROOVY

Seville oranges

Seville oranges are only around for a few weeks in late January and February, but it's good to know that you can put them in the freezer until you need them. The bitter juice is also a very good base for a winter salad dressing.

What with the backpacker going off on her gap-year travels, I almost leave the marmalade-making too late, but am saved by the last boxful of Sevilles at the local greengrocer. Soon the kitchen is a bubbling, aromatic and bittersweet orange fug, the sour orange taste eclipsed by a sweet alchemy all of its own, with just three ingredients: oranges, sugar and water. No wonder DH Lawrence said, *'I got the blues thinking of the future, so I left off and made some marmalade.'*

But even with such literary credentials, I read that in the year to January 2006 the number of marmalade eaters dropped by 400,000, and 80% of consumers are over 45. Maybe it's the grown-up bitter taste of the peel that puts the younger generation off, or its association with crusty old majors stuck behind the *Daily Telegraph* at breakfast. But if you think about it, spreading a piece of decent toasted bread with a golden dollop of proper marmalade is right up there with all that's good about modern eating. Marmalade is an all-rounder, giving orangey flavour to all sorts of things: sauces, tart bases and steamed winter pudding (see opposite) for example. I like eating it, with hard cheese and apples, as a pudding too. Even better if you can make your own or enjoy someone else's batch.

Emma's marmalade

makes 6-8 x 250g (8oz) jars

Emma's marmalade recipe is my favourite. We swap notes and there's keen discussion over whose has the deepest colour, the most bite, and so on.

1.5kg/3lb Seville oranges
granulated sugar
water

Cover about 1.5kg/3lb Seville oranges with water in a large, heavy-based saucepan and simmer until soft – about 1–2 hours, depending on the toughness of the peel. Retaining the liquid, remove the oranges from the pan and cut into halves, scooping out the pips with a teaspoon: a bit fiddly but not too onerous. Return the pips to the pan and boil rapidly for 10 minutes. This extracts pectin to help the marmalade set. Strain the liquid into another bowl and discard the pips.

Using scissors, cut the peel into pieces – bigger ones if you like it chunky and vice versa for a finer texture. I like my slices to be about 1cm (½ inch) wide and 3cm (1¼ inches) long. That's because I like a good proportion of chewy peel. Measure the strained liquid left in the pan and add 500g/1lb/3 cups of peel and 750g/1½lb/3¾ cups sugar to 450ml/¾ pint/2 cups liquid. If I've lost more liquid than normal, either because I've boiled everything for too long or the oranges are not quite as juicy, then I will top up with some water.

Bring to the boil slowly, then boil rapidly until setting point is reached; this is when you get a wrinkly look on the surface of the mixture. I tend to over- rather than under-boil, just so I can be sure to get a good set. This might not be good marmalade practice, but it works for me (see page 178 for tips on jelly and jam making and testing for a set).

Leave the hot marmalade to stand for 15 minutes. Sterlize 8 x 250g (8oz) jars by washing them in hot soapy water and then drip-drying them on a rack in an oven preheated to 140°C/275°F/Gas mark 1. Put the marmalade into the jars, then cover with waxed discs and cellophane lids tied with string.

Marmalade steamed pudding

makes 4 small puddings

(see over)

This is a delicious combination of the bitter flavour of the orange and the sweetness of the sponge.

100g/3½oz/1 stick unsalted butter
100g/3½oz/½ cup caster sugar
2 eggs, beaten
100g/3½oz/½ cup self-raising flour
8 tbsp marmalade (see above)

Substitute the marmalade with golden syrup for a really sweet and sticky winter comfort pudding.

In a mixing bowl, cream the butter and sugar. Add the beaten eggs. Fold in the flour. Grease 4 individual pudding moulds and put a tablespoon of marmalade at the bottom of each.

Add the mixture and cover with greaseproof paper lids tied with string, or a piece of foil fitted tightly. Stand in 2.5cm (1 inch) of water in a roasting tin and place in an oven preheated to 180°C/350°F/Gas Mark 4, for 50 minutes, until risen. Turn out the puddings into serving bowls.

Heat the remaining marmalade in a pan, pour a tablespoonful over the top of each pudding and serve.

ICED GEMS

The new year feels like a fresh start, as I walk through silvery streets in the early hours to meet daughter number two off the free New Year's Eve night bus.

Wrapped up warmly and in thermal socks and clogs, a stint in the garden always clears the head, even if there are piles of dead matter that I didn't quite get rid of before the big freeze began. Iced sugar plums come to mind as I cut the very last rosebuds to put on the table. For the past month I have been delaying, but I must not put off the job of pruning the roses any longer, even for the sight of these pink gems.

My mum showed me how to prune to an outward-pointing dormant bud, making cuts at an angle (with very sharp secateurs) to let the rain run off. This lets the new stem develop and grow outwards, leaving the centre of the plant open.

Good news! Garden experts predict the freezing weather will encourage an explosion of colour as the blanket of snow has put back the flowering of daffodils, crocuses and snowdrops. For the past decade, spring flowers have come up early, meaning the impact of the traditional spring bloom has been barely noticeable. Particularly pleasing to know is that garden pests such as aphids and white fly, which survived the milder winters of the past few years, are expected to have been decimated in greater numbers.

The earth is hard, but I'm not unhappy that the squirrels find it challenging to dig up the tulip bulbs. I will be generous though and put out nuts and seeds for the undeserving beasts.

I don't compile lists of New Year's resolutions because there are too many elements of my life that could do with fine-tuning and better application. I am going to settle for just one: a bicycle. It will keep me fit and get me from A to B in a slow and carbon-friendly way.

INSPIRATION

Food

Beamish and McGlue
461 Norwood Road, London, SE27 9DQ
beamishandmcglue.com
Great for sourdough bread and slices of delicious cake.

Brindisa
Brindisa Shop at Borough Market
The Floral Hall, Stoney Street
Borough Market, London SE1 9AF
brindisashops.com
Spanish olives: Manzanilla, Arbequina; baby capers, Manchego, saffron, Ortiz tined tuna.

Brixton Farmers Market
Brixton Station Road, Brixton,
London SW9 8PA
lfm.org.uk/markets/brixton
Every Sunday 10am-2pm
Biodynamic fruit from Brambletye Fruit Farm, fantastic Norfolk Horn lamb from Dameon at The Sallowes Flock and fabulous fresh fruit and veg from farms in Cambridgeshire, Kent and Lincolnshire.

Café Sintra
Stockwell Rd, London SW9
For a Portuguese experience in south London I drink 'bicas' coffees and enjoy 'Pastel de natas' in this café cum deli.

Franco Manca
Unit 4 , Market Row, London SW9 8LD
francomanca.co.uk
Mouthwatering sourdough pizzas in the hustle and bustle of Brixton Market. Most delicious (well I think so), is the seasonal tomato, mozzarella and basil variety.

Green and Blue
38 Lordship Lane, East Dulwich,
London SE22 8HJ
greenandbluewines.com
Organic and biodynamic wine shop, bar and deli.

Leila's Shop
17 Calvert Avenue, London E2 7JN
020 7729 9789
Fried eggs with sage and other homely delights.

Nick and Joanna Kemp
Breoch Oark, Kirkconnel Estate,
New Abbey, Dumfries DG2
Jf.kemp@quista.net
Dexter beef and Shetland lamb from the couple's herds.

Persepolis
28-30 Peckham High Street, London
SE15 5DT
foratasteofpersia.co.uk
Sweet lemons, pistachios and other Persia in Peckham delights.

Pretty Traditional
47 North Cross Road, London SE22 9ET
prettytraditional.co.uk
Greengrocer and my source of local quinces for making 'membrillo' quince paste.

Tapas Brindisa
18-20 Southwark Street,London SE1 1TJ
tapasbrindisa.com
Tapas of padron peppers and tortilla, Cava, Manzanilla and oaky white Rioja wine.

West Norwood Fishmongers
326 Norwood Road, London, SE27 9AF
Fresh fish from a brilliant woman called Pauline, who saved her local fish shop and continues as a fishmonger at Billingsage fish market. I buy her Cornish mackerel.

William Rose
126 Lordship Lane, East Dulwich,
London SE22 8HD
williamrosebutchers.com
Organic and free range meat (Longhorn Cattle and Aberdeen Angus are specialities), poultry, game and eggs.

Household

Labour and Wait
18 Cheshire Street, London E2
labourandwait.co.uk
My favourite source of timeless functional products, such as watering cans, garden trugs, leather work gloves, pans, aprons and scrubbing brushes.

John Lewis
300 Oxford Street, London W1A 1EX
Johnlewis.com
Everything from wool blankets, crisp cotton sheets and white plates to ironing boards.

Melin Tregywnt
melintregwynt.co.uk
Beautiful blue and white check woven blankets for keeping beds and sofas cosy in winter.

Prices Candles
prices-candles.co.uk
Creamy coloured ones look smart in simple white candlesticks, small candles for sitting in holders to decorate the Christmas tree, and tealights for twinkly summer garden feasts.

Pure Style
purestyleonline.com
My range of simple and utilitarian blue and white striped Irish linen tea-towels and blue and white enamel bowls and basins.

T.G Green
tggreen.co.uk
Blue and white striped 20s style Cornishware mugs, plates and bowls.

Tobias and the Angel
68 White Hart Lane London SW13 OPZ
tobiasandtheangel.com
Good for vintage, Welsh blankets and simple block printed fabrics in great colours.

Volga Linen
17 Langton Street, Chelsea, London
SW10 0JL
volgalinen.co.uk
This is the site to visit if you want to treat yourself to the most divine linen sheets. I will when all my brood have left home.

Where I go for making things

John Lewis
Everything for craft and sewing plus a very extensive range of sewing machines.

Hobbycraft
Stores countrywide
hobbycraft.co.uk

Paper, pens, glues, glitter and everything for being crafty.

Ian Mankin
271-273 Wandsworth Bridge Road,
Fulham, London SW6 2TX
ianmankin.co.uk
Striped cotton ticking and great plain cottons for curtains, blinds, loose covers, cushions and upholstery.

MacCulloch & Wallis
25-26 Dering Street, London W1S 1AT
macculloch-wallis.co.uk
All the bits and pieces for sewing, plus great cotton ginghams.

VV Rouleaux
261 Pavilion Road
Sloane Square, London SW1X 0PB
vvrouleaux.com
Just about any type of ribbon is found here, including rick rack and flamenco-style bobble trims.

Paint colours

Cuprinol
cuprinol.co.uk
Good colours for outside. Willow is my favourite garden fence shade.

Earthborn paints
earthbornpaints.co.uk
Environmentally friendly clay paints in muted colours. My attic looks good in Paw Print, a sludgy earth coloured shade.

Farrow & Ball
farrow-ball.com
Parma Gray and Teresa's Green are two great timeless shades for walls.

Little Greene
littlegreene.com
Paint colours including my favourite Citrine green shade. Look out too for its paler sister, Pale Lime which is a great mood lifter in a north facing room.

Retro

Caravan
3 Redchurch Streret, Shoreditch, London,
E27 DJ7
caravanstyle.com
Emily Chalmers interprets flea market style in her treasure trove store.

Midcentury Modern Shows
Dulwich College London SE21 7LD
ourshowhome.com
From an Eames rocking chair to an Ercol table, this is is really good event for picking up mid century furniture and accessories at good prices.

Sunbury Antiques Market
kemptonantiques.com
Country furniture and other excitements.

Garden

Allotment
National Socity of Allotment and Leisure Gardeners Ltd
nsalg.org.uk
All about allotment gardening.

Association Kokopelli Organic Seeds
terredesemences.com
Over 2,500 varieties of organic seeds.

Brockwell Park Community green houses
brockwellparkcommunitygreenhouses.org.uk
Chillis and other seeds.

Crocus
crocus.co.uk
Everything from parrot tulip bulbs to lavender and fruit trees.

David Austin
davidaustinroses.com
900 varieties, including my favourite Gertrude Jekyll and Constance Spry blooms.

Fallen fruit
fallenfruit.org
Public fruit jams and nocturnal fruit forages.

habitataid.co.uk
Native plants & seeds, classic apple varieties.

Ironart
ironart.co.uk
Romantic garden arches in metal mesh.

De Jager
dejager.co.uk
Bulbs since 1868.

Organic Gardening catalogue
organiccatalog.com
Organic composts and fertiliser.

The Real Seed Catalogue
realseeds.co.uk
Heirloom & open pollinated (non-hybrid seeds).

Thompson &Morgan
thompson-morgan.com
Garden supplies, beans, peas and other seeds.

Urban Bees
urbanbees.co.uk
Bringing bee-keeping to the city.

More online inspiration

Etsy
etsy.com
A source for buying the crafty and handmade.

Nordljus
nordljus.co.uk
Delicious travel and food blog.

Remdolista
remodilista.com
Brilliant sourcebook for the home.

Shedworking
shedworking.co.uk
All about sheds and shed people.

Slowfood. slowfood.com
Good food and the pleasure of eating.

White Terraces
whiteterraces.com
Simple, white and beautifully restored interiors to rent in Olhão.

INDEX

REFERENCES

1 (p9)   Honore Carl, *In Praise of Slow*, Orion, 2004
2 (p22)   Haymans Edward, *The English Cottage Garden*, 2004
3 (p62)   Pavord Anna, *The Tulip*, Bloomsbury, 1999
4 (p69)   Clover Charles, *The End of the Line*, Ebury Press, 2004.
          © Charles Clover 2004. Reprinted by permission of Random
          House Group Ltd
5 (p86)   Crawford Ilse, *Sensual Home*, Quadrille, 1997
6 (p89)   Bissell Frances, *The Times Cookbook*, Chatto & Windus, 1993
7 (p101) David Elizabeth, French Provincial Cooking, Penguin, 1970
8.   Eastoe Jane, *Wild Food*, National Trust Books, 2008

9 (p135) Humphries John, *The Essential Saffron Companion*,
          Grub Street, 1996
10 (p164) Keats John (1795-1821), *To Autumn*
11 (p181) Boggiano Angela, *Pie*, Cassell Illustrated, 2006
12 (p193) Slater Nigel, *Real Cooking*, Michael Joseph, 1997, © Nigel
          Slater. Reproduced by permission of Penguin Books Ltd
13 (p198) Lane John, *Timeless Simplicity*, Green Books, 2001
14 (p205) Hartley Dorothy, *Food in England*, Macdonald, 1954. Quote
          taken from paperback edition, Piatkus, 2009. © Dorothy
          Hartley

BIBLIOGRAPHY

Boer Nick, Siebert Andrea, *The Algarve Fish Book*, Edition Marisol, 2005

Carluccio Antonio, *A Passion for Mushrooms*, Pavilion, 1980

Clifford Sue & King Angela, *England in Particular*, Hodder & Stoughton, 2006

Conran Terence, *Design and the Quality of Life*, first published by Thames and Hudson 1999, The Ivy Press

Davidson Alan, *Mediterranean Seafood*, Penguin, 1972

Davidson Alan, *Penguin Companion to Food*, Penguin, 2002

De Boton Alan, *The Architecture of Happiness*, Penguin, 2007

Festing Sally, *Gertrude Jekyll*, Penguin, 1993

Hambro Nathalie, *Particular Delights: Cooking for All the Senses*, Norman & Hobhouse, 1981

Larkom Joy, *The Salad Garden*, Frances Lincoln, 1984

Maeda John, *The Laws of Simplicity*, Massachusetts Institute of Technology, 2006

Marie-Pierre Moine, *The Cooks Herb Garden*, Dorling Kindersley, 2010

Minns Raynes, *Bombers and Mash: The Domestic Front 1939-45*, Virago, 1999

Norman Jill, *Make Do and Mend*, Michael O'Mara Books, 2007

Nilson Bee, *The Penguin Cookery Book*, Penguin, 1952

Pizarro José, *Seasonal Spanish Food*, Kyle Cathie, 2009

Phillips Roger, *Mushrooms and Other Fungi of Great Britain and Europe*, Pan Books, 1981

Phillips Roger, *Wild Food*, Pan Macmillan, 1983

The Gardening Year, Reader's Digest, 1969

Roden Claudia, *Mediterranean Cookery*, BBC Books, 1987

Sevilla Maria José, *Spain on a Plate: Spanish Regional Cookery*, BBC Books, 1992

Shepherd Sue, *The Surprising Life of Constance Spry*, Macmillan, 2010

Spry Constance, *Simple Flowers*, J.M.Dent, 1957

Stuart Tristram, *Waste: Uncovering the Global Food Scandal*, Penguin, 2009

Stein Rick, *English Seafood Cookery*, Penguin, 1988

Wiseman John 'lofty', *SAS Survival Guide*, Collins, 1993

Watson Guy Baxter Jane, *Riverford Farm Cook Book*, Fourth Estate, 2008

ACKNOWLEDGEMENTS

This is my sixth book – and a joint endeavour with Vanessa Courtier. It has been a pleasure to work with Vanessa, whose brilliant talents for photography and design have made this book the one I'm most proud of.

Of course, the whole project would never have come to fruition without Polly Powell, Chief Executive at Anova, and Anna Cheivitz, Associate Publisher at Pavilion, who saw the potential in the sample pages that we brought into their offices one dank November afternoon. Thank you. I must also say a huge thank you to the team at Pavilion, who've worked so hard and enthusiastically to nurse the book though all its stages. Rebecca Spry's editing has kept me on my toes, while Jenni Davis and Jackie and Jane Moseley have been similarly demanding and professional. Georgina Hewitt's work on the book's design has also been excellent.

Then there's the team at home: my family: Alastair, Tom, Georgia and Grace, who are quite superhumanly supportive when I am working on a book. Not flinching, for example, when asked to hold up light reflectors in an uncomfortable position for a picture or to be the tasters and guinea pigs for recipes.

Special thanks, too, to Grace for her simple and beautiful illustrations. I must also thank Patricia Gill for all her support and creative skills in the Pure Style office, and Miranda Schwartz for working on the cover design.

More thanks and gratitude to my husband Alastair, to Emma and Damon Heath, Fiona and Simon Wheeler, Katrin and David Cargill, Ilse and Oscar Pena, Tessi and Jonny White, and all the friends and family who have been sources of inspiration in my cooking. And, as always, thanks to my agent Clare Conville for support and words of wisdom. Finally, thank you to Rachel Whiting for allowing me to include the photograph on pages 244 and 245.

Pictures on pages 212, 215, 220 and 265 by Jane Cumberbatch.